The Uncollected Bau

The Uncollected Baudrillard

Edited by
Gary Genosko

SAGE Publications
London • Thousand Oaks • New Delhi

First published 2001

SAGE Publications Ltd
6 Bonhill Street
London EC2A 4PU

SAGE Publications Inc
2455 Teller Road
Thousand Oaks, California 91320

SAGE Publications India Pvt Ltd
32, M-Block Market
Greater Kailash - I
New Delhi 110 048

British Library Cataloguing in Publication data

A catalogue record for this book
is available from the British Library

ISBN 0 7619 6530 0
ISBN 0 7619 6531 9 (pbk)

Library of Congress catalog card number available

Typeset by SIVA Math Setters, Chennai, India
Printed in Great Britain by Athenaeum Press, Gateshead

Contents

Acknowledgements

This collection would not have been possible without the strong support I received from Jean Baudrillard. Much to his credit, Monsieur Baudrillard was nonplussed by my resurrection of texts from very early in his career, from a period which may be called, to use the same term by which early works by the young Marx are informally known, the 'prehistoric Baudrillard'. Although the 'posthistorical Baudrillard' is much more well known, there is much to be said for and learned from the bridging operation.

Since many previously untranslated works are included here, I would like to thank the international team of translators without whose skills and persistence and generosity this volume would not exist. In alphabetical order, they are: Peter Flaherty, Ben Freedman, Mike Gane, Paul Hegarty, Thomas Kemple, Mark Lajoie, Nicole Matiation, Paul Patton, Sophie Thomas and Timothy Dylan Wood. Existing translations by Paul Foss, Joachim Neugroschel and John Johnstone, Hans Eberstark and Jan Avgikos, are also included. I would like to personally thank Pascal Boutroy for his assistance regarding the delicacies of French correspondence.

The assistance of Brian Singer as a translation consultant was invaluable, as was the advice offered by Chris Turner.

Gary Genosko,
Lakehead University, Thunder Bay,
Ontario, Canada

Introduction

Gary Genosko

> Have I actually wiped away all the traces, all the possible consequences of this book? Did I reach a point where nothing can be made of it; did I abolish every last desire to give it a meaning? Have I achieved that continuity of the Nothing? In that case, I have succeeded. I have done to the book what the system has done to reality; turned it into something no one knows what to do with any more. But something they don't know how to get rid of either.
>
> *Cool Memories III* (Baudrillard 1997a: 140)

The goal of this collection is not to produce a new picture of Baudrillard; a picture that nobody – including Baudrillard himself – has ever seen but should see or, for some reason or another, could not see until the publication of this volume. I have not uncovered secrets about Baudrillard or works that are so out of character that Baudrillard will henceforth appear strange to himself and, of course, to us, his readers. This will not have been a scandal. We don't need another French *affaire*; neither are the essays in this volume old favourites that I have dressed up in a new jacket with a visible label, like all those academics who have forgotten to remove the labels on their raincoats and price tags on their shoes, in the manner of the quotations and notes in their conference papers (Baudrillard 1997a: 17).

Indeed, this is not an exercise in depth hermeneutics by means of which I may claim to have discovered more in Baudrillard's work than anyone else, even Baudrillard. Rather, this volume contains *uncollected but unforgotten* essays by Baudrillard from the 1960s forward, but with two emphases: on radical political reflection from the 1970s and urban sociology in the broadest sense from the 1960s; yet things are never quite as plain and simple as they seem.

Every reader of Baudrillard and his critics and interlocutors knows the importance of the trope of forgetting: forgetting someone's discourse in particular (Foucault) as a critical form of revealing it to perfectly mirror the object (power) it unknowingly legitimates and extends; another call to 'forget' in the form of a dismissal – of Baudrillard, no less, as a pseudo-critical imperative, a tired postmodern swipe; and the binary partitioning of the word as an expression of divided loyalties: for(get) Baudrillard; and even the reminder of *sans oublier Baudrillard* – let's not forget him, ok? – as a backhanded form of critical acknowledgement. There are undoubtedly more examples, but I have forgotten them. No, it is not a struggle between infinitive and imperative; of spacing and brackets; not even one of last-minute inclusion, no matter how knowingly it may have been used.

These are unforgotten essays; essays that have not been, on the whole, subject to forgetting in any of the aforementioned senses. They are not new, though only a few have appeared in English before this publication; some are actually fairly old and date from the late 1950s and early 1960s before Baudrillard became *Baudrillard*. Almost all of them have been at least mentioned in bibliographies of Baudrillard's writing; so my claim is not to originality, or even to wily archival work. Only one or two of the most well-known pieces have been the object of concerted critical reflection, at least in the English-language literature.

How did this collection come about? The answer is deceptively simple. It is a wish list. Whose wishes, you may be wondering? I canvassed a number of senior and junior researchers in the field and asked them to list the top ten or so articles by Baudrillard that they would either like to see translated and in print or rescued from out-of-print publications. All of the lists were remarkably similar because everybody knew in advance which articles – and versions – were at issue before I had even posed the question. These articles were, then, never really forgotten, just uncollected; they waited patiently until they would again see the light of day in another language and in some cases in another format. If there is anything new in all of this it is that these texts are freshly unforgotten after languishing for too long in the bibliographies of obsessive researchers. Still, not everyone will be satisfied, especially those who always think there is more to come or that I haven't dug deep enough, been thorough enough, or that I will probably end up publishing his shopping lists.

Unforgotten: between forgetting and remembering the project becomes one of *re*collection and the work itself involves sorting through the obvious choices. The articles in this book do not even have the charm of having been lost; lost *and* found is perhaps more accurate in its paradoxicality. They were there all along and everybody concerned knew it. There is nothing to be revealed about the identity of Baudrillard that was not already known in one way or another, if merely signalled by the bibliographers among us. Yes, we may need a biography of Baudrillard, but you won't find it here.

Every reader of Baudrillard knows his critique of residual meaning as an anti-symbolic principle (latent, hidden, repressed, remaindered, something meaningful) from the perspective of the symbolic in his particular use of it; Baudrillard (1993: 230) argues, using the poetic and comic as his examples, for that which is totally resolvable with nothing left over and nothing behind it, either. It is in this spirit that I offer this (un)collection. There is only intense enjoyment in an exterminating symbolic exchange; unforgetting is not a game of resurrection. It is a game of exchange among readers of Baudrillard in which a limited number of obscure articles (those on the aforementioned wish lists) are critically consumed in a little 'potlatch' of research. This is an offering in exchange for those wish lists, among other gifts. And our milieu, our professional symbolic order, involves the exchange of texts, sharing and contesting ideas, and developing new concepts. A book like this one will probably never have immense sign value as a result of being fetishized – like *America*, for instance – even though many books by Baudrillard have met this fate. But this merely illustrates what Mike Gane (1991a: 84) pointed out some years ago: symbolic exchange and sign consumption are interwoven despite Baudrillard's desire to take the position of the former against the latter. The publishing economy of sign exchange and exchange value combines with the gift exchange among researchers and readers, critics and friends alike. There are still all of those offprints and author's copies to do something with, after all.

Those who would criticize my selection might do so from the vantage point of surplus value and the alleged affluence of research materials (there is always more to be discovered or I have held something back to increase the power of my position). This would threaten the delicacy of reciprocity and institute separation in the form of a hierarchical relation of power in which I held the decisive card by getting to the source first, or finding what hitherto could not be found. This is why I have insisted that these essays are *unforgotten*, lost *and* found, already (t)here. But in returning this volume as a counter-gift, I cannot fail to enter into a game of cancellation in which it is impossible for me to assume such a position of power. Baudrillardian symbolic exchange cancels authority and institutes the obligation to respond as its fundamental rule. Not only the obligation of giving, but of receiving as well, and returning in kind as its own end; no departmental dirty tricks and no long knives; no holding out against the competition or racing to the publisher.

Recollection and exchange is a matter of elimination – elimination by publication, elimination through celebration, editing as an act of liquidation; as Baudrillard put it with regard to psychoanalysis: 'the real *analytic* operation *eliminates its object* which comes to an end in it' (1993: 204). The object at issue is not, of course, Baudrillard. Rather, it is the object of knowledge (of these texts by Baudrillard that I have chosen and organized and presented in a specific way under the sign of an original editorial impulse and contribution to the literature because they were in some manner 'missing'), mastery of which it is assumed that I, editor-expert, possess and will actualize, and perhaps continually prop up by some promotional means. Mastery is relinquished in the symbolic circuit and the subject of knowledge is cancelled in his object of knowledge. This is an intensely pleasurable experience, Baudrillard suggests, and it is the kind of expenditure in which nothing remains to be accumulated; residues would be the uncancelled seeds of power in this scenario. The remainderless, as opposed to the remaindered, book: this would be the 'continuity of Nothing' about which Baudrillard wrote above with reference to the third volume of his *Cool Memories*. Collections like this one are, in this sense, like collections of fragments because perhaps they will one day amount to nothing and in so doing demonstrate the Baudrillardian reversal of meaning and nothingness. For what is lacking in overall coherence and the development of ideas, exhaustive developmental perspective and critical insight will be regained in delicacy, lightness, banality, brevity, and laziness.

The terms of this offering are both limited and severe. Limited in the first and second instances by the number of texts at issue and by the relatively small audience interested in such matters only for whom this introduction was written with the presupposition of a certain sensitivity to the symbolic in Baudrillard. But severe in the sense that the disavowal of mastery and the idea of cancellation in the symbolic circuit, making it impossible to claim that this book reveals the secret identity and desire of Baudrillard or the hidden topic of his work, also entails that it is not possible to use the work as a critical hammer or even as a tool of a feigned indifference ('By the time it came out I'd lost interest ...'). The work enters into a social relation and thereby loses its self-centredness; its fullness emptied, its latency evacuated, its meaning no longer radiating across the literature, resolution is achieved and, with it, laughter and enjoyment.

A few issues remain. To those (Zurbrugg 1997) who would position Baudrillard as a photographer[1] without reference to his cut-and-paste construction of quotations for Swiss-born René Burri's collection of photographs *The Germans* (from 1963, the year after he came into contact with the post-war German avant-garde group of artists known as Gruppe '47, numbered after the year of its founding in 1947, the year of the Marshall Plan, and whose members, and enemies, included the cream of the literary crop – Böll, Grass, Weiss; the latter's plays Baudrillard translated into French, etc.), there is a selection from Baudrillard's own accompanying text on German character and culture. Burri's *The Germans* was a European version of Robert Frank's *Americans*. Baudrillard's text is almost entirely made up of quotes, with a few motifs that hint at his later preoccupations: he uses the two editions (*orientale* and *occidentale*) of the Duden dictionary to look at definitions of key words: atheism, individualism, democracy, idealism. The contrasts are extraordinary. There is a remarkable section entitled 'Inanimate Objects: Do They Have a Soul?' in which Baudrillard notes that talking cigarette machines regale you with a 'Vielen Dank! Auf Wiedersehen' after a successful purchase, and eiderdown has a way of slipping off the bed during the night; these are intimations of his theory of the revenge of objects that he developed later in the decade. Nestled amongst the quotations by authors from many nations are a few by German novelist Uwe Johnson (1934–84), whose work, in French translation, he reviewed in 1962 for *Les Temps Modernes*.

One of Baudrillard's preoccupations at the time was the representation of the two Germanies, a motif that was acute in Johnson's life and work since he fled the East for the West in 1959 after the publication of his first book, which was thought to be too critical. In Baudrillard's review essay, he describes Johnson's method – the objectivity of description of functional things which are 'the perceptible form that the collectivity takes' – as an *artisan's Marxism*. We are so accustomed to the later Baudrillard's descriptions of the antiquation of history with the 'vague terrain' created by the fall of the Berlin Wall – 'I stand before this wall with astonishment, and I no longer manage to remember anything' (1989: 35–6) – that these interests, while technically unforgotten, seem not very cool at all. Previously uncollected works can be, in fact, quite hot.

There is always the temptation, of course, to read the early Baudrillard through the lens his later work and thus invest the former with all the dominant trends and interests of the latter; yet there is little to be learned by this, but bathing the uncollected in the golden light of decades of refinement and international fame is a way to raise its status. Luckily, there are few examples that suggest nothing of the sort. In the critical reviews of Calvino and Styron, Baudrillard warns against the charms of the former's style (subtle and accomplished, yes, but forced and passive, as well) and the latter's excessive baroque formality. In his book reviewing – a practice, after all, of retelling someone else's story – unlike his translation work on German literature, which points beyond itself, Baudrillard's work is limited and provides little fuel for overinterpretation. Still, when Baudrillard mentions his work on Brecht's *Dialogues d'exilés* with Gilbert Badia, circa 1965, in a much later interview, it is to underline this point: 'I will never read them again, but their influence remains with me in other ways' (see Gane 1993: 180).

The translation, almost thirty years after the fact, of Baudrillard's important early books on consumer society, *System of Objects* (1996) and *Consumer Society* (1997), not only provides a frame for the investigations into the development of his approach to mass-mediated life, thereby situating him alongside Barthes as a key thinker of the maturation of French consumer society, but also give a renewed sense of urgency to the task. For it becomes clear that the range of work – on McLuhan, Lefebvre, Marcuse, urban sociology of *Utopie*, and more properly sociological topics such as anomie, masses, and social control – was acutely insightful and tightly structured; that Baudrillard was, in fact, *engaged* with critical theory. It is also clear that he absorbed most from those he criticized severely and thus may be said to have read most closely: McLuhan (the pitfalls of the medium theory of communication) and Lefebvre (the troubled relation between technique and mass culture). But reading Baudrillard presents one with the paradoxical fusion of perspicacious *and* disputatious claims in the same stroke, just as certain methods seem to collude with and justify the system they criticize (indeed, it may be said he learned this lesson about structuralism from Lefebvre and applied it to McLuhan's media theory through an analysis of the latter's categories such as hot and cool and his technological model of galaxies). And this is precisely what created the conditions for Baudrillard's groundbreaking analysis of the political economy of the sign: the recognition of structuralist formalism as an ideology detectable at the heart of its smallest elements at the level of the sign. Moreover, like Lefebvre, Baudrillard went deeply into structure and technique and then manufactured a way out, with Lefebvre it was a dialectical critique of structure with several variations, the efficacy of which Baudrillard was not convinced, and with Baudrillard, symbolic exchange. The semiotic analysis of repression flows from this: police and play/repression and regression (i.e. the repression of adult desire by regressive, pre-genital advertising [infantilization] whose return haunts the sexually liberated by diverting them from really transgressive sexual irruptions by providing the signs of this for their amusement); ultimately, then, a semioticized Marcuse. It was then by pushing hard on these simulations of cyberneticized consumer society that Baudrillard defined for himself what may be called a method: take drugs, for example, since they are taken as a result of pressures secreted by a fully integrational, overrational system. Drug-taking is not marginal or deviant. Rather, a highly developed society's overcapacity for order produces anomalies and, as it tries to rid itself of them, produces more. This is the 'perverse logic' of the so-called 'drugs problem'. Baudrillard's little essay written for the *UNESCO Courier* should have been held up against the hysterical 'War on Drugs' that raged through America during the 1980s like a placard: it's this so-called 'war' that ensures drug-taking will not only continue, but intensify.[2]

The question of Baudrillard's aesthetic production does not end with photography. His string of poems 'Stucco Angel' appears here for the first time in translation. As translator Sophie Thomas notes in her preface to the piece, the sound shape of the original is irrecoverable in English. This is both inevitable and exemplary as far as the general Baudrillardian thesis of the remainderless message is concerned. This makes the medium the message, as it were; the fact that English cannot capture the alleged anagrammatic dispersions of phonic elements of the names of key thinkers, according to Gane's (1991b: 121ff.) demonstration, is complemented by what such a demonstration must surely admit given Baudrillard's interpretation of the anagrams of De Saussure against the grain (his insistence on the annulment of the theme-word or name rather than its recuperation; rearticulation is acceptable, but reconstitution is not). It is fitting, then, that this is lost in translation.

But there is, for the avid bestiarist, something else at play here: a veritable menagerie of animal life populated by circling buzzards, white-tailed eagles, blackbirds, swallows, and cocks, not to mention spiders, pigs, dogs, wild cats, and butterflies. As an undisciplined theorist (Genosko 1998), I have insisted on the extravagant interpretive practice of tracking the animals that are put to work in theoretical texts. They may have been hitherto unnoticed but they have certainly left their marks. Indeed, the notion of the 'bestiary' was a key word that Gane introduced into the Baudrillard literature, but which was not yet oriented toward its proper quarry. Baudrillard has done a great deal to clarify this matter in some of his fragments: 'Where they get all excited about "natural resources" and conviviality, I get excited about these pretty, translucent scorpions ...' (Baudrillard 1997a: 40). On a biographical note, these poems may be the oldest pieces of writing in this collection, dating from the 1950s (Gane 1991b: 122).

Perhaps more biographically relevant are the selections published here from the political commentary 'The Divine Left', the last major piece of Baudrillard's *oeuvre* left to be translated as a piece. Reading the sections of this political diary-like account of the rise and fall of the French Union of the Left in the late 1970s and early 1980s is like, to borrow a phrase from Thomas Kemple (1995: 241, n. 16), 'reading Marx writing' in an *uninhibited* manner because it is so obviously a sensitive satire of the *Eighteenth Brumaire*, from the periodizing right down to the inhibitions of reading political events: Marx's spectres are mediatized by Baudrillard as the monster from *Alien*; instead of the 'iron death mask of Napoleon', we find the funereal visage, the gloomy ecstasy, of Mitterrand; the emphasis on fiasco is the salient point, however. This is Baudrillard's contribution to the many faces of Marx (the Little Girl, the libidinal beard, the severe thinker, the scientist, Young Hegelian, etc.) in postwar French intellectual life. If Marx once complained of emasculating German translations of French slogans (Kemple 1995: 221, n. 7), 'interpretive castration' is not the French – Baudrillard's – interpretation of Marx, even though castration is on the cards for the French Communist Party. Even if Baudrillard mixes his sources together, borrowing a ghost or two from the *Manifesto* as well, it would be incorrect to reduce this work to a burlesque commentary on French politics and the vicissitudes of the Left in particular.

The first section is animated by events in Italy, by the 'historical compromise'. To borrow a coinage from Pier Paolo Pasolini from the early 1970s that he used to describe the anti-democratic network of power established and fortified by the

Christian Democratic Party in Italy, as well as the opposition parties which colluded with it, *Il Palazzo* ('The Palace'), it may be said that counter-hegemonic struggle requires that 'The Palace' be put under renovation! With the compromising 'historical compromise', *compromesso storico*, of 1973 (to 1978) in which Enrico Berlinguer's Communist Party entered 'The Palace' with its traditional enemies the Christian Democrats, thus becoming a *Partito di Governo* rather than a *Partito di Lotta*, little hope remained that renovations would ever get under way. The second reference to the Italian situation is to Gianfranco Sanguinetti's (aka 'Censor') *True Report on the Last Chance to Save Capitalism in Italy* (1975; partial translation, Censor 1980), in which the compromise is said to be 'solely for the communists' and the alleged perils of the 'revolutionary' Italian Communist Party (ICP) entering the sphere of power is an illusion exported by the ICP itself. This piece of Situationist agitation in which the ICP will be forced to make those who refuse to work do so appears in the guise of an enemy, a lion, like the carpenter in a *Midsummer Night's Dream* who allows part of his face to show through his costume: don't fear, it's me, I am no threat! Baudrillard's interest in the Italian situation, in the 'historical compromise', the Red Brigades, and the flowering of the Autonomy movement, is not confined to this text. A few years later in 'The Beaubourg Effect', he would remark at the end of the essay:

> In Italy something of the same type is in play. In the actions of students, Metropolitan Indians, radio-pirates, something goes on which no longer partakes of the category of universality, having nothing to do either with classical solidarity (politics) or with the information diffusion of the media (curiously neither the media nor the international 'revolutionary' movement reverberated with the slightest echo of what went on in February-March of 1977). In order that mechanisms of such universality cease functioning, something must have changed; something must have taken place for the effect of subversion to move in some sense *in the inverse direction, toward the interior, in defiance of the universal*. Universality is subverted by an action within a limited, circumscribed sphere, one that is very concentrated, very dense, *one that is exhausted by its own revolution*. Here we have an absolutely new process.
>
> Such indeed are the radio-pirates, no longer broadcasting centers, but multiple points of implosion, points in an ungraspable swarm. They are a shifting landmass, but a landmass nonetheless, resistant to the homogeneity of political space. That is why the system must reduce them. Not for their political or militant content, but because, nonextensible, nonexplosive, nongeneralizable, they are dangerous localizations, drawing their uniqueness and their peculiar violence from their refusal to be a system of expansion. (1982: 12–13)

The description of this implosive, non-extensive, decentred turning inward of subversion and the particularization of the universal seems to be lifted right off of pages penned by Félix Guattari about the same events; yet with Baudrillard the consequences of this ironic process (the inward collapse of the idea of revolution which is more potent than revolution itself) are incalculable, while for Guattari they were valorized as molecular politics, new forms of collective belonging and expression with both anti-capitalist and anti-socialist deterritorializing potential, without a plan or distinct programme for the future. Guattari believed that the molecular revolution, the necessity of which follows from his bald statement

'There will be no more October revolutions', will not take place through traditional political organizations but, on the contrary, 'will be a generalized revolution, a conjunction of sexual, relational, esthetic, and scientific revolutions, all making cross-overs, markings and currents of deterritorialization' (Guattari 1980: 236). Baudrillard's passing reference to the events of March 1977 (of course, later in September there would be mass arrests of professors, including Antonio Negri, closing of editorial houses, etc.) – mass demonstrations by workers and students and unclassifiable urban radicals ending in riots in the streets of Bologna as the communist mayor called in the police in armoured cars, the events of which were broadcast by the pirate radio station, Radio Alice (after the events of March it was closed) – are discussed by Guattari (1977) in detail. Both Baudrillard and Guattari, however, put the emphasis on the 'originality' of these events; as Guattari once remarked, 'the inventiveness and intelligence of the Italian militants are absolutely astonishing' (1978: 184). Unlike the enthusiasms of Guattari, Baudrillard is content to connnect this originality with the implosive form into which meaning disappears. Although this is not the occasion on which a complete investigation of the personal and professional relationships between Baudrillard and Guattari may be undertaken, suffice to say it was during the late 1970s that their editorial projects led them to the Parisian suburb of Fontenay-sous-Bois, home of both Cahiers d'Utopie, which published Baudrillard's *À l'ombre des majorités silencieuses* (1978a) and *Le P.C. ou les paradis artificiels du politique* (1978b), and Éditions Encres/Recherches, publisher of Guattari's *La Révolution moléculaire* (1977) and *L'Inconscient machinique* (1979) Both *Utopie* and *Recherches* were journals in which Baudrillard and Guattari, respectively, had a longstanding interest.[3]

These are, then, the sources for Baudrillard's account of the rupture of the French Left's 'Union of the Left' strategy engineered by Mitterrand, the first secretary of the Socialist Party (SP) he established in 1971. The Union between the Socialist Party and the French Communist Party (CP) secured an impressive victory in the municipal elections of March 1977 which seemed to create the conditions for success in the parliamentary elections which were scheduled for the following year. However, the CP's escalation of criticism aimed at its partner, the SP, flared after March 1977 and the CP's leader, Georges Marchais, insisted on an advanced and comprehensive programme of social expenditures and nationalization of major industries, ultimately including their subsidiaries, thereby undermining the Union's public position in an economic statement released just before Mitterrand would debate President Raymond Barre on television. In a subsequent meeting Marchais would reconfirm his commitment to the Union, while still insisting on pushing forward the CP programme; at the SP Congress at Nantes, Mitterrand called for immediate negotiations with the CP. But this was the beginning of the end as Marchais condemned the Congress. By August, the game of attack and non-reponse (Mitterrand) was well advanced and by September at the Left Summit of Mitterrand, Marchais, and Robert Fabre, leader of the Mouvement des Radicaux de Gauche (MRG), the CP leader was mouthing hardline slogans like 'make the rich pay' to his Socialist partners whom he criticized for selling out to the Right. Mitterrand mustered a reply: the CP holds the keys to defeat. By the end of September, the Union had broken apart and the CP had, as it was often remarked, snatched defeat from the jaws of victory.

Baudrillard presents the CP as a 'dissuasion machine' incapable of winning power and, in fact, he praises it as a party not of loss but of radical losers who throw the election. This notion of radical losers was celebrated elsewhere in his work (Baudrillard 1981: 204) with reference to the same images of Poulidor – 'the eternal runner-up whose fame is derived precisely from this chronic incapacity to wrap up victory' – and the long-distance runner in Alan Sillitoe's *The Loneliness of the Long-Distance Runner* (1959), a Borstal Boy who, as a form of revolt, throws away certain victory in a race sponsored by his reform school. I have suggested elsewhere (Genosko 1999: 60ff.) that this is nothing less than Baudrillard's theory of sports involving a fundamental symbolic ambivalence about performance and perfection in competition: to sell oneself short against every rational demand to do otherwise. Now, taken in a political context, one simply cannot claim that Baudrillard's procedures for reading the events of French politics are straightforwardly cynical or overtly anti-communist, or any of the typical criticisms directed at him by Kellner (1989) such as 'unfair' or 'ill-tempered'. Rather, they are uninhibited translations of Marx's writing in the *Brumaire* and suggest there is something radical, something symbolic, about irresistibly botching it.

The March elections of 1978 witnessed a record turnout of voters and an increase in the CP's representation, alongside the SP's, MRG's, and Left independent's losses, and a disastrous second ballot, the result of which was that the Right won the elections no matter how one counted: by percentages or seats. Giscard d'Estaing had dashed Mitterrand's personal hopes. All of a sudden, the elections of 1981 loomed large on the horizon. And, like a gigantic special effect, on 10 May 1981, Mitterrand was elected president. This analysis is conducted by Baudrillard in terms of his reading of the silent majorities as an implosive mass-form whose behaviour is unpredictable. There is, then, a fairly close identity between the Beaubourg essay and this section of 'The Divine Left' to the degree that the building and the Left are 'monuments of cultural dissuasion' and simulation into which the masses throw themselves not out of the desire to acquire something, but to participate in the collective act of mourning the death of politics and culture; this sort of participation is the last shovel of earth, as it were, on culture and politics. If there is a lesson here it is that Baudrillard's Beaubourg essay and 'The Divine Left' can be reread together in order to deepen one's understanding of his theory of the mass-form through cultural and political examples.

Baudrillard has also fulminated against the Right in France, with most of his vitriol directed at Le Pen. Political bankruptcy has occurred on the left and right. My interests here run from the French Left through terrorism in Germany – Baudrillard's interpretation of the skyjacking to Mogadishu, the murder of kidnapped industrialist Hans Martin Schleyer, and the imprisonment, trial, and ultimately the deaths of the 'gang of four' of the Baader–Meinhof Group who were in the high-security prison of Stammheim (Ulrike Meinhof, Andreas Baader, Gudrun Ensslin, Klaus Röll). It is once again constructive to read Baudrillard together with Guattari on these matters. Guattari's essay on the collective film by stellar West German filmmakers (Alexander Kluge, Rainer Werner Fassbinder, *et al.*) *Germany in Autumn,* which deals with the aforementioned events in Germany, is a study in contrast, as several scholars have noted (Rentschler 1990: 40, n. 56). Baudrillard analyses the events in terms of the spectacular media violence released by the terrorist acts themselves, a violence whose effect is to inject ambivalence into the events and erase distinctions between terrorists and prisoners; the implosion of meaning in the media which calls into question the distinction between the truth of events and their mediatic simulation, in other words. Guattari (1996: 182) takes the side of Kluge and Fassbinder and their attempt to 'counteract this collective intoxication by the media'. Still, despite these marked differences, the issue remains how one theorizes the collective affects (melancholia) released by media coverage of terrorism, whether in Germany or Italy.

For Guattari it is a mistake for those involved in armed struggle to reproduce this collective guilt, whereas for Baudrillard there is no room for political critique of the sort Guattari advances; it is not possible to speak of 'mistakes' but only of the symbolic strategy of terrorism whose actions force the State and the media to overproduce 'true' records of events to such a degree that they both overheat because of their own excesses. This is the Baudrillardian strategy of drawing the 'system' onto the symbolic plane, disorienting and denying the surety of its coordinates by pushing it beyond itself.

Recall that it has often been observed by those interested in the relationship between local and national politics and immigration in France that the CP, through its local governments and mayors in areas often notable for their large concentrations of North African immigrants in public housing (explained as the 'ghettoization' of workers' housing), adopted openly restrictive policies with regard to the distribution of diminishing social services – first (from the late sixties to mid-seventies) protesting the inability of their constituencies to absorb more than a fair share of immigrants, and later using quotas to restrict access to housing and education. At the national level, however, it was Marchais who deployed the issue in the presidential elections of 1981, even going so far as to support the local mayor, with the additional support of the SP, in an attack on a 'ghettoized' workers' housing unit in Vitry, a Paris suburb, with a bulldozer. Only two years later the National Front of Le Pen would lift this thin veil of racism and fascism and exploit at the national level the connection between immigration and other issues such as unemployment, crime, inflation, and post-colonial national identity (Shain 1985: 185–6).

Throughout his readings of American visual artist Barbara Kruger and New York-based Swiss painter Olivier Mosset, Baudrillard diagnoses the incoherence of the contemporary scene in a series of ironic disorders: the medium of Kruger's work no longer believes in its message, a play on McLuhan's famous buzzphrase, but still wants to communicate even after there is nothing left to say. In the case of Mosset, the task of painting (Neo-Geo Abstraction) is to find the means to represent this indifference itself, to paint the void without filling it with anything other than its own nothingness. These examples of Baudrillard's art criticism highlight his philosophical celebration of reticence in the face of the facile multiplication of simulated communications as a style perfectly adapted to contemporary conditions.

Perhaps most important, though, are the Baj pieces. Enrico Baj, the Milanese painter, has been active in the European art scene since the early 1950s, when he promoted the 'End of Style' Manifesto of the Nuclear Movement (promoting *tachiste* and surrealist methods; many years later in 1983 he wrote the 'Static Futurism' Manifesto in favour of sleep, slowness, peace and quiet, equality of the sexes, and sun) against right angles, Geometric Abstraction and machines and militarism; later in the mid-fifties he collaborated with Asger Jorn in the Situationist International on work directed against the 'New Bauhaus', and eventually established, alongside Man Ray, Arturo Schwarz, and others, the Milan chapter of the Collège de Pataphysique, the Institutum Pataphysicum Mediolense. Despite their differences, Baj may be counted among Baudrillard's fellow pataphysicians. What Baudrillard celebrates in Baj's work is the monstrosity of the paint itself and not what his figures represent; of course, the overt anti-militarism of Baj's seminal mid-sixties works such as *Generals* and *Military Parades* does not interest Baudrillard as much as the way the materials themselves absorb the violence and brutality of their referents and manage to become 'mythic operators' whose potency lies in their ability to resolve this violence. This is, without question, an imaginary solution of the highest order.

Having worked through the contexts in which this diverse selection of material may be productively and intelligently read, the trope of forgetting that has haunted the critical literature may begin to be rethought as unforgetting. This is my hope for this volume: that it is unforgotten by those who restrict the 'early' Baudrillard to *System of Objects*; by those who would forget his beginnings as a Germanist, a fiction reviewer and, critical theorist; and, especially by anyone uncritically referring to him as a 'disciple' of McLuhan, an apolitical postmodernist, or any of the typical reasons for forgetfulness.

Notes

1. On the question of photography and Baudrillard, one may read Marité Bonnal's *Passage* (1986) – written the same year as Baudrillard's *Amérique* and with the same itinerary, at least at the outset, and for whom he acted as photographer – as a key novel of sorts in which the mysterious 'J' is constantly excited and fascinated by the desert into which he disappears.

2. This essay, dating from 1987 (*UNESCO Courier*, July: pp. 7–9), is not included in this collection since it is scheduled for republication elsewhere.

3. In my *Baudrillard and Signs* (1994: 166–8, n. 2) I devoted a lengthy note to Baudrillard's early work with the *Utopie* group. Together with the influence of Lefebvre, this was the source, I want to underline, of his urban sociological perspective. I am greatly indebted to Richard G. Smith for chasing down all of Baudrillard's articles in this little journal, from 1967 to 1977. I would like to add, however, that Baudrillard continued to collaborate with his colleagues from the early days of *Utopie*, Isabelle Auricoste and Hubert Tonka (1989), on urban architectural issues in the late 1980s, such as those concerning Parc-Ville Villette. During this time Baudrillard also showed a great deal of interest in the architecture of Jean Nouvel (Goulet 1987).

References

Auricoste, Isabelle and Tonka, Hubert (1989) *Parc-Ville Villette*, with a 'Préface' by Baudrillard, Paris: Les Éditions du Demi-Cercle.

Baudrillard, Jean (1978a) *À l'ombre des majorités silencieuses*, Fontenay-sous-Bois: Cahiers d'Utopie.

Baudrillard, Jean (1978b) *Le P.C. ou les paradis artificiels du politique*, Fontenay-sous-Bois: Cahiers d'Utopie.

Baudrillard, Jean (1981) 'Concerning the Fulfillment of Desire in Exchange Value', in *For a Critique of the Political Economy of the Sign*, trans. Charles Levin, St Louis: Telos, pp. 204–12.

Baudrillard, Jean (1982) 'The Beaubourg Effect', trans. Rosalind Krauss and Annette Michelson, *October* 20: 1–15.

Baudrillard, Jean (1986) *Amérique*, Paris: Grasset.

Baudrillard, Jean (1987) 'A Perverse Logic', *UNESCO Courier*, July: 7–9.

Baudrillard, Jean (1989) 'The Anorexic Ruins', in *Looking Back on the End of the World*, trans. David Antal, New York: Semiotext(e), pp. 29–45.

Baudrillard, Jean (1993) *Symbolic Exchange and Death*, trans. Iain Hamilton Grant, London: Sage.

Baudrillard, Jean (1996) *System of Objects*, trans. James Bendict, London: Verso.

Baudrillard, Jean (1997a) *Cool Memories III, 1991–95*, trans. Emily Agar, London: Verso.

Baudrillard, Jean (1997b) *Consumer Society: Myths and Structures*, London: Sage.

Bonnal, Marité (1986) *Passage*, Paris: Galilée.

Censor (1980) 'What the Communists Really Are', trans. Richard Gardner, *Semiotext(e)* [Italy: Autonomia] III/3: 92–5.

Gane, Mike (1991a) *Baudrillard: Critical and Fatal Theory*, London: Routledge.

Gane, Mike (1991b) *Baudrillard's Bestiary: Baudrillard and Culture*, London: Routledge.

Gane, Mike (ed.) (1993) *Baudrillard Live*, London: Routledge.

Genosko, Gary (1994) *Baudrillard and Signs*, London: Routledge.

Genosko, Gary (1998) *Undisciplined Theory*, London: Sage.

Genosko, Gary (1999) 'The Joy of Defeat', in *Contest: Essays on Sports, Culture and Politics*, Winnipeg: Arbeiter Ring, pp. 60–3.

Goulet, Patrice (1987) *Jean Nouvel*, including an 'Entretien avec Jean Baudrillard et Jean Nouvel', Paris: Electa France.

Guattari, Félix (1977) 'Des millions et des millions d'Alice en puissance', in *La Révolution moléculaire*, Fontenay-sous-Bois: Recherches, pp. 377–84.

Guattari, Félix (1978) 'À propos de la répression en Europe', in *La Révolution moléculaire*, Paris: Union Générale d'Éditions 10/18, pp. 179–90.

Guattari, Félix (1979) *L'Inconscient machinique*, Fontenay-sous-Bois: Encres/Recherches.

Guattari, Félix (1980) 'Why Italy?', trans. John Johnstone, *Semiotext(e)* [Italy: Autonomia] III/3: 234–7.

Guattari, Félix (1996) 'Like the Echo of a Collective Melancholia', trans. Mark Polizzotti, in *Soft Subversions*, ed. Sylvère Lotringer, New York: Semiotext(e), pp. 181–7.

Kellner, Douglas (1989) *Jean Baudrillard: From Marxism to Postmodernism and Beyond*, Stanford: Stanford University Press.

Kemple, Thomas (1995) *Reading Marx Writing: Melodrama, the Market and the 'Grundrisse'*, Stanford: Stanford University Press.

Rentschler, Eric (1990) 'Remembering Not to Forget: A Retrospective Reading of Kluge's *Brutality in Stone*', *New German Critique* 49: 23–41.

Shain, Martin A. (1985) 'Immigrants and Politics in France', in *The French Socialist Experiment*, Philadelphia: Institute for the Study of Human Issues, pp. 166–90.

Sillitoe, Alan (1959) *The Loneliness of the Long-Distance Runner*, London: Pan.

Zurbrugg, Nicholas (ed.) (1997) *Jean Baudrillard: Art and Artefact*, London: Sage.

PART I

YOUNG BAUDRILLARD

The Novels of Italo Calvino

Three of Calvino's novels have been translated to date: *The Cloven Viscount, The Baron in the Trees*, and *The Nonexistent Knight*. The first tells of the remarkable fate of two halves of a cavalier split by a cannonball. One of these returns to its native land and spreads terror in the countryside, splitting everything it finds, beings and things, in two. The other follows, repairing the damage as best it can. But the good half is revealed to be as injurious as the damned soul: evil exists in duality. The end is Hoffmannesque: the two halves fight a duel, cut each other again and then, reunited, give birth to a normal man. Apart from Pamela the shepherdess, there are no other characters. The framework is very simple: it is the survey of a given, fantastical, situation; a taste for surprise and for a certain horror, which comes lightly from the pen of Calvino; a cruel fantasy of baroque literature. *The Baron in the Trees*, though in the same key, has a wider aim. A young nobleman of the eighteenth century, threatened with eating snails, flees to the tree-tops, and doesn't come down again for the rest of his life. This flight is the sign of extreme singularity, but not of rupture: Cosimo flies over the world, but from close up. From branch to branch, he keeps his distance from the world, but retains his curiousity, his passion, his taste for happiness. In a slightly caricatured form, Calvino offers us a whole art of living. And the symbol of exile in the trees is richer to the imagination than the scissiparity of the viscount: it takes hold because it is at once natural and absurd. Calvino pushes it a bit too far at times, and certain epsiodes are superfluous. But this 'Robinsonade' [Crusoe] is an improvement over the comic fantasy of the first book.

The Nonexistent Knight follows the same line: to treat, through an absurd but novelistic representation, a schema of radical alienation. After the duality of consciousness figured by the two halves of the body, after refusal in an arboreal solitude, we now have the absence of the body, the being emptied of its substance, because this knight is nothing but a suit of armour sealed around nothing. But he still has heart and prestige, and if he doesn't exist, he is nevertheless there like everyone else, his absence barely surprising those around him. Thus, here again, the story comes from a bizarre plot, and the tone is always that of a chronicle faithful to the absurd – a fantastical detailing, lively and free, and with an ease that is undoubtedly dangerous. One reads it with pleasure, because the substance of the book is more in its fantasy than in its meaning. It is necessary for us to see if this amounts to more than a literature of pure charm.

The epoch of *The Cloven Viscount* is uncertain: it is the war against the Turks. The scene of *The Baron in the Trees* is set against the revolutionary, Napoleonic wars in Italy. With Calvino, history is outlined from far enough away to be an exotic backdrop, but one senses that the concern with it is real, something other than reference, and in a certain sense the characters reflect this. Here, it is the height of the era of chivalry: Charlemagne and the Moors, battles and revelries, the Amazon Bradamante and the priggish knights, the peasants and the Order of the Grail, nothing is missing from the theatre of chivalry, nor of what goes on in the wings, for the idealism of the *chanson de geste* is naturally cut through by the slightly nutty realism of cartoons. Bradamante pisses in the river, Charlemagne peels his crayfish, high virtues disappear behind those of the kitchen, and Gurduloo the squire, the buffoon who turns himself into a duck or a pear tree, is Sancho Panza turned Pinocchio.

Our Don Quixote, the Nonexistent Knight, has undergone the same stylization: he is nothing more than a suit of armour, which is white as a sign of purity, but also of abstraction. And which has nothing inside: this is chivalry sublimated, and nearly puppet-like. Agilulf Bertrandin of the Guildivern became a knight for having preserved the virginity (in spite of herself) of a girl: he himself will keep, all his life, this character of virtuous uselessness and maniacal perfection. His inexistence still has some grandeur, but it is fundamentally as much a bygone as the maidenhood it protects. He is a valiant knight, an ageless paladin, glacial, and all the more so since the chronicle of his deeds and gestures is benign. He has nothing left in him of an adventurous chivalry (that is for Raimbaut, the naive and impetuous one, of whom we will speak again); he bears the ritual, methodical phariseeism of a caste henceforth without value. We see the tired emperor, his barons partial to blazonage and cabbage soup, going mechanically to war bereft of ideas. The ceremonial is everywhere immutable, but fundamentally, everything goes haphazardly and no one cares. All that amounts to nothing more than boredom and moroseness – an empty concept, of which Agilulf is the sign. But there it is: he himself takes everything seriously, he doesn't sleep, he settles every detail, he checks the sauces, he buries the dead. He whose flesh has vanished from his armour, his soul also passes into the dogmatism of organization. He is a maniac. Cosimo also, the Baron perched in the tree-tops, ends in a bit of delirium, but it is that of an adventurous exuberance. Agilulf, though, is an abstract maniac.

There is nevertheless a kind of drama about Agilulf: in a discreet way, he is nostalgic for his body. Perplexed, timid, haughty, pensive – this empty armour sometimes exudes tenderness, regret for a real life. This goes even to the point of anger: he fights against bats (derisory, but so alive), while moonbeams and gusts of wind pass over him. Only once in the book will he make a gesture of affection, when he caresses the hair of Raimbaut. Perhaps he had been formerly, or dreamed of being, a hot-blooded knight, of flesh and heart? But he recovers himself quickly and becomes pure lucidity again: 'He, Agilulf, always needed to feel himself facing things as if they were a massive wall against which he could pit the tension of his will, for only in this way did he manage to keep a sure consciousness of himself'.

But this ascetic rule is not without prostration. Agilulf suffers from time to time, which nuances the metaphysical nature of his character.

All of Calvino's heroes are in a more or less metaphysical position. Cosimo is too, though, from his perch, he watches the world and follows its ways with passionate interest. The Knight is less romanticized: he is but an inverse reflection, slightly veiled, of chivalry. Thus, the episodes don't coalesce around him with the same force that they do around the figure of the Baron, who imposes the active, vital symbol of an escape lived out in the trees, while Agilulf is more a passive allegory of absence. From this comes the novel's greater exteriority – less force, but more freedom. We are here in a game of chess: each piece has its course, along a thread that is sometimes broken, but the whole is clear and seductive.

But if we succeed in reading this novel with pleasure, is it too much to demand of a book that its power to warn be sought out, that it specify its basic limits? I don't think so. Now, this Knight poses a problem. Let's take the scene with the widow Priscilla: this woman whom he believes himself to have saved by a hard-fought struggle had herself put in motion the dangers he overcame. Heroism remains sincere, but it is empty – things have changed. Moreover, he cannot possess this woman because he is disembodied, and what is the prestige of his armour worth if he cannot get out of it to possess the woman, and the world? (Gurduloo, on the other hand, that ill-formed being, takes the maids one after the other.) Thus, the story's irony draws from the uselessness and the historical, baroque aspects of chivalric values, and this is good. But Agilulf is something else again: a positive hero, by the admiration that Raimbaut and Gurduloo bestow on him, but above all through the love of Bradamante – by the subtle eroticization with which Calvino surrounds this absent form, this nothingness, this Don Quixote under x-ray. And not only Bradamante but Priscilla, at the end of her sexless entanglement with the empty armour, appears more beautiful than ever.

This is more serious since Calvino is himself caught up, I think, with the magic of nonexistence. As long as he brings before us his ironic marvels, the reader is satisfied: we feel ourselves to be amused, and lucid. But once women begin to dream of the Knight, the perspective changes. We read even a story as 'distant' as this affectively, and the desire of a woman is always equivalent to the idealization of a hero (in *The Baron in the Trees*, too, all the women are excited by the solitary hero). And what is it that is exalted, sublimated, romanticized, here? It is the disenchanted emptiness of the end of a clan; it is the subtle bitterness of emptiness and of impotence. To take it in the modern sense in which the book concerns us, it is the political disenchantment with action, the evanescent, and the abstract singular.

This is signified by, among other things, the final, romantic Assumption of the Baron in the trees, who leaves nothing more behind him, in the hands of the petits bourgeois represented by his brother, than empty land. In *The Nonexistent Knight*, we have a historical option: faced with the Knights of the Grail, that veritable gang of the True Blood of Jesus, the peasants rise up, organize themselves, and recover their land; Torrismund, a disillusioned knight touched by 'class consciousness', heads up the peasant militia. In this way, too, the Baron condescends to help the revolutionary armies from his tree-top. Here, though, the historical opening is even less convincing. Not only does Calvino develop it on the fringe of his hero, whose quintessence distances him from real struggles, but it is unable in any case to draw its truth from a style of legendary morality. The lively, schematic descriptions, the light turn of phrase, the multiple – pompous or 'popular' – usage of dialogue, favour the baroque imagery of the majority of episodes; they are perfectly suited to a battle of Franks and Saracens, but certainly not to a peasant insurrection against the plundering commandos of the Grail. This dissonance is indicative of a forced solution and, on the level of the work, a stylistic fault. But the two are connected: there is no transition between the unusual (even the happily unusual), and real history.

Here, we touch on a limitation of Calvino's novels: their real irresolution, in spite of their charm. Agilulf in his armour, like Cosimo in his trees, travels the world with pride and both are brought down without leaving traces. Their paladin other-worldliness is certainly ironized by the author, and is thereby brought back to life for us. But the fact of a disillusioned, narcissistic ideal remains, of which the playfulness of style itself is the sign.

The eccentricity of Gurduloo, the squire, is the exact inverse of that of the Knight: the one confuses himself with every living creature, and even with inanimate things, while the other has withdrawn from the world and from himself. The one exists without knowing it, the other doubts everything, but doesn't exist. The one is unlimited carnal confusion, the other pure form sealed in armour. The contrast intended by the author is too strong not to fall into allegory. They are two themes that confront each other without lively cohesion, two poles if you will, angel and dervish, that sustain the maximum distance of the story but without empowering it. There again, from the simple point of view of invention, the Baron is better situated because he unites in one figure these two eccentric tendencies: sublime bias and natural exuberance. The fable works better in this way, and whereas we feel that Gurduloo's folly is too intended by the author – his animal or vegetable incarnations create the effect of a forced imagery – his character remains perhaps more metaphysical still than that of Agilulf.

Finally, the greatest sincerity and appropriateness of style in Calvino is found with characters who are properly romantic, who are impassioned, heroic, and very Stendhalian in their ardour and their particularity. Such are Pamela, from *The Cloven Viscount*, and above all Viola, from *The Baron in the Trees* – tender, imperious, uncompromising, without human respect, and who, even in her disguises and masks, is in the lineage of the Lamiels and the Minas of Wanghel. Bradamante has the same proud and amorous temperament. From admiration first for the Absent Knight, Agilulf, she will move toward the more normal love of the Living Knight, Raimbaut. It is this evolution that seems closest to the meaning of the book, and to the 'truth' of Calvino: the surpassing of absence and the will, toward a realized happiness. Thus, an art of living. That Bradamante is at the same time the reclusive nun who writes the chronicle, the reflexive face of the book (one thinks of *The Spanish Military Nun* of de Quincey), confirms the Stendhalian nature of her character: its playful ardour and lucidity. It is through her that Calvino speaks.

From his side, Raimbaut – young, fresh, enthusiastic – takes up certain traits of the young Cosimo and recalls Fabrice: he discovers battle, the world, women.

His admiration for the Knight is, all the way through the book, parallel to Bradamante's, and it is this common admiration that separates them, because she is devoted to an absent and ambiguous ideal. Once this is effaced, they recover the simplicity of passion and of happiness. A charming conception, a bit frail and schematic in the absence of real drama, a bit anachronistic in the context of the modern novel, but why not let it be? Faced with nearly all our novels where singularity plays continually on unhappiness, Calvino's playfulness describes again, as did Stendhal's, a singularity of happiness.

Insofar as the novel, particularly the modern one, can be said to be the literary form of absence, *The Nonexistent Knight* takes up this fundamental theme: it 'incarnates' absence, but in a light and fantastic way. A crisis in values is staged, played with, parodied. Calvino doesn't aim at radicalism, and we are a long way from the objective novel; or rather, Calvino would be the azure-tinted, illustrated form, full of bravura and Italian brio, of the same crisis of absence that haunts our northern novel. We will not reproach him for not having 'emptied' the question. The limitation is rather in the complacence of style: one cannot see where it could lead him, if not to other pleasant books. It lacks aggressivity.

The story itself resembles a happy hunt: to the pleasure of writing, which one feels clearly through the pleasure of reading, is mixed the secondary satisfaction of the decor, of the facts and gestures of the past. In this way, too, Jules Laforgue, in his *Moral Tales*, closely linked the humour to the desuetude of his characters. There is, in Calvino, a species of surrealism, of a highly cultivated fantastic, that has lost all aggressivity: a sign of extreme culture, but also of flight. The background in his novels is always that of a historical end – the decline of chivalry, the last decades of the Ancien Régime – because it is there that 'the art of going hunting each morning for happiness' becomes all the more surprising, and so, for the writer, does the hunt for images. Through this background, our own epoch is indicated, but avoided at the same time. There is only one urgency for Calvino: that of happiness, and in that, it's every man for himself. But, insofar as this happiness is first of all for Calvino in the charm of writing, we feel that something of this charm is worn out today, and that Calvino is aware of it too. One feels it in the veiled nostalgia of the tone, which is the very one that the Knight feels toward the absence of his body. And Calvino states it clearly through the nun who composes the chronicle, this being a judgement upon himself and a warning to us not to trust too much in his charm: '*One can never be sure of saving one's soul by writing. One may go on writing with a soul already lost*'.

Translated by Sophie Thomas

Note

Originally published as 'Les Romans d'Italo Calvino', *Les Temps Modernes* 192 (1962): 1728–34. Review of the French translations from the original Italian: *Le Vicomte Pourfendu*, Paris: Albin Michel, 1955; *Le Baron Perché*, Paris: Le Seuil, 1960; *Le Chevalier Inexistant*, Paris: Le Seuil, 1962. The English translations are: *The Non-Existent Knight and The Cloven Viscount*, trans. Archibald Colquhoun, New York: Random House, 1962; *The Baron in the Trees*, trans. Archibald Colquhoun, New York: Random House, 1959.

Review of William Styron's
Set This House on Fire

Two epigraphs in the most pure visionary style, both baroque and Puritanical, introduce Styron's two books. Even if the 500 pages of the first, *Lie Down in Darkness*, are without hope, destroyed by alcohol and guilt, the second, *Set This House on Fire* takes us well beyond the neurotic splendour of the Southern mentality, in terms of both meaning and general tone. We are reminded at times of Faulkner, Tennessee Williams and even Fitzgerald, but ultimately we are far from the fantasy worlds of metaphysics or the flowering perfume of death, hysteria, and languor, and especially of a certain aristocracy of a lost generation. Styron is always baroque while remaining vital. We are conscious of a health, a breath, a firm hand as well as a certain naïveté, that of a new generation, plebeian, that is apparently trying to join together heaven and hell, rather than illustrate evil through the absurd. In flamboyant terms, it is a healthy reason that speaks, and using a relevant framework for analysis. Less genius, more application, we are reminded also of Dostoevsky, and Styron often takes the same risks; but he feels no dread and we can travel to the depths with him and return unharmed.

In a village in the south of Italy, a rich and idle American, Mason, rapes and indirectly kills a young Italian peasant girl, Francesca. Cass, an alcoholic and unsuccessful artist who plays the clown for his wealthy patron, avenges the young girl by killing Mason. But it is only later that we learn of this act, this is not the end of the book, and the actual truth only comes to light slowly through the stripping away of guilt in the confrontation between Cass and Leverett, two years after the murder. There is forgiveness for crime in the soul of those who live through it, and when the book opens, the fate of Cass and Leverett is hidden. What has happened has yet to take place. The story is about lifting the veil on the experience of guilt, and in a completely different manner than that of a mystery novel: these are real facts that must find a place; once revealed, the latent meaning of Mason's murder must resolve the present situation between Cass and Leverett. This is the argument put forth in the book; not the simple recounting of a violent act, but a genuine essay of applied psychology.

The scope of the novel comes from how this applied psychology fits into a historic trial, in which the list of charges is laid out in the first pages by Leverett's father. It is an unpitying denunciation of Yankee deculturation, of the American myth embodied in every bank, every Esso station, every stone and every soul of the little town in Virginia where Leverett spent his childhood. And not only there, but also outside the physical boundaries, this pharasaic power spread across the four corners of the globe, this Marshall Plan that confirms the slavery of the rest of the earth – all of this is symbolized by a sort of baptism of evil, just before the tragedy, when Di Lieto is run over by a sports car, and later, when Mason drives a Cadillac into this Italian village that has been reduced to a sort of film set. It is a modern replica in reverse of the arrival of the first Blacks to Virginia one morning in 1619, it is the original sin of the violation of humankind that runs from age to age but the inevitability of which now seems to be specifically American. 'What this country needs', says the father, 'is that something happens, something fierce, like what happened in Jericho or Sodom ... so that people, having been through the crucible of hell, become human again'. What will happen to this country is inscribed in the personal fate of Mason and Cass: rape, murder, descent into the flames and the return from hell. The sin, the historic fate of all peoples is analysed, reconstituted, and surpassed in the psycho-drama Mason–Cass–Leverett. And Styron, at the outset, because he wants to get to the bottom of the problem, goes beyond the contradiction of bad faith, to what has always served to cover the original sin: the opposition of South to North. Mason is Virginian on his mother's side and wealthy on his father's: which means that all the money of the North only served to illuminate the complex burying and guilt of the South. For the first time, this civilization is tried in its entirety and, with it, the truth of white domination.

Wealth is insolent and breeds loneliness. If Styron gives so many children to Cass, and even a last child, a symbolic one, as a post-script, it is to emphasize the sterility of Mason. Around Mason, everything is dry, even the women wither. It is both despite his charm, his good looks, his fortune, and because of them that Mason is an end in himself: others turn to him and he fails to meet their needs, he cannot feel his wealth except in a world impressed by it. He lives in this Italy that he detests because it is a victim, his simple presence as a rich Yankee lord is a perpetual rape: 'These Italians that we shower with money and that still steal us blind ...'.

Behind the handsome Mason lies the Bursar's Office of Naples. He supports artists, but he himself is supported by the army. And this parasitic relationship is fully realized in both human and sexual terms. Any energy is good for the taking to redirect towards evil. What one might call a 'provocative' existence. Flexible but sterile, talkative but insensitive in a country where beauty is a gift from heaven, Mason can only provoke others in an attempt to frustrate them in turn. And so, he makes Cass sign his obscene painting and engages in pornography to liquidate his complexes. And all the stories that he tells, this intense bluffing, his flattery, his tenderness, are all signs of the complete destruction of his heart, which can only serve to question the conscience of others. In this way Yankee history is expressed through Mason: 'He pillaged an entire continent, stripping away its resources, its flora, its fauna, its beauty'. He is the expression of the triumphant guilt of the North, that which transcended the mad justification of money by the guilt-ridden suffering in the South, 'for having spit on the back of their black brother'. It is the impact of these two different forms of guilt, the triumphant guilt of Mason and the suffering guilt of Cass around the 'black' virginity of Francesca, that brings about the tragedy of this book.

Wealth without work burns the conscience and is transformed into Aggression, which in the case of Mason is pushed to the extreme of rape. Excessive wealth becomes 'a famine without a cure, breeding fever in a man, shaking him up and tormenting him and leaving violence as his only refuge'. The rape scene reflects this in a characteristic manner: it is above all an act of sexual pathology, but one that occurs in a psycho-historical context. It is his bitterness at having been robbed by Francesca that unleashes Mason's aggression. What would he have done with what she stole? Yet he reproaches her compulsively, he provokes himself unrelentingly, pushing Francesca deeper into the very thing that made her steal from him in the first place: misery – and at the same time his own guilt about his wealth. He, in all his wealth, can only be robbed; she, in all her nakedness can only be raped: a double obsession in which Mason locks himself, and where puritanical sexuality is intertwined with pathological racism. Of all this Cass is the unfortunate conscience.

There is an almost literal parallel to be made between Mason and Stavrogin in *The Possessed*. In both cases the drama centres on the sterile and provocative power of what is perhaps an immense force that is held back by guilt, negativity that shortly becomes evil. The story in both books, from beginning to death, focuses on the double rape (the oyster merchant's young daughter, Francesca; the little girl who is hung, Lisa). And like Stavrogin, Mason is handsome. A particular physical beauty that is tied to this transcendence lacking in energy and that drags down all who approach, as a function of their own inverted and guilty energy, in an identification that is largely sexual. This is the case with all the characters of *The Possessed*, in particular with Shatov, much like Leverett, and especially like Cass. In this manner, even Mason's bluff is perceived to be a favour, a caress (Leverett is astonished by the story of the Yugoslav resistance, Cass is fulfilled by the false praise offered by Mason for his paintings), and when Cass or Leverett decide to denounce him, it is again turned against them. Pleasing and humiliating at the same time is Mason's art. 'He inspires a mixture of anger, shame, resentment and at the same time a warm and degrading gratitude'. It is therefore difficult to settle up with him, his guilt is triumphant, he is too handsome to be doubted: 'each time he becomes himself again, desperately plausible from head to toe'. Parasitic handsomeness, caught in a trap, inverted, and who wants to catch others in it, Mason evidently can only seek his own death – it is difficult to reach Mason, to approach his truth: like a white surface, he reflects guilt. He is not an incarnation of evil, that would be too simple. Only murder can save others from Mason and him from himself.

The only thing left in the world that Mason cannot take but must be given is death; this is what he really wants from Cass, and in the end, this is what he obtains lovingly from him as he runs away along the edge of the cliff, in a landscape that is suddenly liberated with a faunlike freedom. Because this murder is a deliverance, it won't be atoned for but rather elucidated later: this is the theme of the book. What cannot be atoned and remains unsaid, because that which is the source of evil, sin itself, like an ancient fate, cannot be told, is the murder of Francesca by the idiot.

The problem of evil and the sharing of guilt dominates this book. The problem is posed by Cass: can man be separated from evil and be saved (if we were to take away this and that in Mason's personality he would be a swell fellow), or in certain cases is man evil himself and must man and evil be destroyed together? In the past even horses were hung. Today all is justified. Did Cass have the right to kill Mason?

Styron offers a concrete response to this moral question. While evil is described in absolute and almost theological terms, as is the case until about half-way through the book, guilt cannot be forgiven. Guilt comes into being through the telling of the tale itself, when the formal opposition of good and evil is resolved in the ambivalent experience of the Cass–Mason relationship. In the past, on the day he participated in the destruction of a Negro cabin, Cass was forced into evil, his soul became an accomplice: his soul trembles with violence and with having been violated. There he is, sent from his own land, to Europe, and alcohol: he is looking for his enemy, the one who forced him into evil – Mason. And Mason is looking for Cass, the one he can hurt and through whom he can hurt others, and for whom the humiliation will testify to the power of his money: the cursed coupling of two parts of a single split conscience. Right from the beginning, Cass loses possession of his name: Mason calls him Kasz. Already the spirit of evil slips in through this crack, and is firmly established when Mason favours Cass with a bottle of whiskey.[1] Cass accepts it like a 'nice warm cowpie', the secret and bitter jubilation, like in the scene at the cabin, of being violated and, through his collusion, all the Blacks, all the colonized, all the miserable beings – Michelle and Francesca. They are the third character, the one on whom pure evil is exercised. Because Styron is right in recognizing that violence, like Oedipus, is a story with three characters. A 'Third World' is necessary so that Mason can possess Cass, and Cass needs this in order to be free: under pressure from Mason he responds by defending Michelle from death, to the rape of Francesca he responds with murder. Because from then on, all the obsessions with runover dogs that must be destroyed, with Black women (whether in the mourning dress or with dark skin) sagging under burdens, with this ferocious misery around him, crystallize into a fantasy of a sadistic God and a wild fit of autodestruction – all this that Cass has dragged along since his birth is incarnated in Mason the second he touches Francesca. It is he, Mason, this monstrous tarantula, 'this depraved black God, that seems coldly resolved to annihilate his creatures'. He gets rid of him, then, with love almost as one would put a suffering creature out of misery, and by identifying with him as someone who could have raped Francesca also. Cass's attitude, because it is so pure, is not clear: if he doesn't sleep with Francesca it is because he is obsessed with his fear of raping her: 'Mason, the bastard, he did it, he did it to her', says he with hate and admiration. And it is for this reason that Cass kills Mason as if he were exorcizing a part of himself.

The ambivalence between Cass and Mason is absolute. It is a novel without women. Francesca is an object of guilt and Styron does not make us believe that she is real. The other women are dolls, the sexuality attached to them is nothing but empty obsession. It is that sexuality with its murderous conclusion, its authenticity integrated into the Cass–Mason relation, in the rivalrous relation of guilt over the same sexual object, both the real and symbolic Francesca. But their sexuality is not exactly homosexual.

It is because Styron has understood well the living dialectic of evil that can go beyond atonement and open a living dialectic around the resolution of evil. Already Luigi[2] reproaches Cass for his excessive feelings of guilt. It is word for word what the Bishop Tikhon reproaches Stavrogin for in the latter's confession just before his suicide. Only his good words do not stop Stavrogin from committing suicide, nor Cass from spending two years prostrated in the 'forgetting' of the murder: no one can become guiltless alone. And so, Styron wants to bring us to the conclusion of all guilt not through redemption, which he no longer believes possible, but according to a method of applied psychology. This is when Leverett intervenes. In fact, this is when the book begins.

Cass acts to bring all of the latent immemorial guilt incarnated in Mason to the highest point of open guiltiness, that of murder. This violence is cathartic, Cass is able to shed his shame. But all the possibilities that this murder opens up are blocked by the guilt attached to it. Nothing is won yet. Cass no longer drinks, but his actions remain a dead transcendence that oppresses him. Leverett must come and force Cass to retreat, thus accomplishing the ultimate step, the elucidation of murder. We see how he can do so: he was present during the adolescence and death of Mason, he dreamed of this death (his projected dreams of murderous friends), he almost killed Di Lieto, his story runs parallel to that of Cass. We can see elsewhere why he is necessary: because there must be a witness, and not a neutral one, but one who is susceptible to transference, with a conscience to render guiltless (Cass–Leverett) as there must be a perverted conscience to exercise evil (Mason–Cass).

Leverett is not simply a confidant-detective telling the story, characterized by average values and carried away by a contagious fate. On the one hand, like the coryphaeus and the chorus in Greek theatre, he is the mass of people, the universal audience with the exceptional fate of the few. On the other hand, he is the liquidator of the immense dispute that the rape of Francesca signifies for all of civilization and the unconfessed, unsolved crime committed by Cass against Mason. His fiancée lost, his native village defigured, his father without hope, the failure that is his daily life and that of millions of others, and for which the epigraph is the magical transcription, this is the incriminating evidence in a trial that he will lead between himself and Cass and Mason: through his active investigation, it is chance and the decline of heroes that joins with that of the people. In him the work takes on its entire essence, its objective intention, the finality of humanness. Is the book really successful? Leverett himself does not appear particularly sympathetic to us. But what gives moral weight to the book is not Cass's last child or the resurrection of Di Lieto (too symbolic), but, rather, the perspective of total edification. This is also the function of tragedy: to make a people aware of its monstrous origins, rather than a performance of mythological crimes as we prefer to see.

This is the primary difference between *Set This House on Fire* and *Lie Down in Darkness*, a blind book, without air, heavy and brilliant with unresolved incestuous guilt: everyone unrelenting in their obsession, the father with alcohol, the mother with hate, the daughter with sex. While excellent, the book is interminable. Styron took seven years to write the next, but the jump is decisive. This time it breathes. The truth is at the end of the book. Violence goes beyond itself. Everything is organized. A bit too much at times.

The unresolved crime of the War of Secession, like that of Atrides in the Greek tradition, the original murder and the perpetuation of evil, this infantile fatalism radically mythologized by Faulkner, unsolveable and frozen in the lack of understanding of the defeat of the South, materialized in the empty air of the South and outside of time, this fatalism is exposed here in historic, dramatic and psychological terms that are those of its solution. The patriarchal, refined puritan décor of the Southern novel, this violence focused on the Black presence, has fallen. Paris, Rome, Naples, Sambuco, New York, Virginia, the trajectory alone opens the book to a present-day world almost politically up-to-date. Blacks are no longer Blacks, but rather all the miserable peasants of the world: Michelle and Francesca. This redeems the racial debt.

Styron especially redeems the theological or puritanical debt of evil: the slow elucidation of murder reveals that there is no longer an individual or racial fate but rather a shared behaviour, an exchange of guilt, a lived responsibility. We merit others and others merit us. A analytical and human resolution of evil can stem from this applied psychology, through a new exchange: Cass–Mason is resolved by Cass–Leverett. Styron makes evil a violent performance but takes away any dramatic conclusion; he goes to the limits of guilt and back again. His intention is evident in the organization of the book. There is no one hero. The hero is Mason until the middle of the book, as long as it is a question of Mason's death, then Cass is the hero when it is explicitly a question of murder. This jagged line from which emerge, often from the depths of childhood, the fragments of present reality, this broken progression, does not come from a terrorist use of memory, nor from a gratuitous explosion of space and time: Styron is not a trickster. On the contrary, the progressive inscription in memory of the crime always brings one back to the present. The writing does not attempt deliberately to create a sense of unreality either, it does not suspend fate, it stays close to the story (it has a tendency to shrewdly use melodrama). Elsewhere in Styron's work there is humour, a jovial inspiration and especially (beginning with *Lie Down in Darkness*) a particular talent, often related to grass, clouds, the time of day, and the effects of alcohol, for conveying the slightest trials and tribulations of mood, this part of us, both shadow and light, that flees from morning to night, a whole impressionism of guiltiness and mental fragility – different from the novelistic style, and that compensates for the elaborate and theatrical architecture of the whole.

Because it must be admitted that it works too well. Absolute success would have been achieved if Styron had not padded his book, watching too carefully over the plot, and using all means to consciously write a polished work of art. In this way the figurative and the exaggerated take away at times from the drama: all that is Italian, landscape and characters, the beauty and the misery are relatively conventional, although seen pathetically through Cass's conscience; Leverett remains floating, carried by intention. A too careful use of composition means that the framework is never laid bare, but embedded in a context that is no longer tragic but rather symbolic or spectacular, becoming excessive in certain scenes, such as the description of Cass's neurosis. The book lacks irregularity, the sudden revealing that characterizes a style. Certainly it can be said that in reference to the book's intention, that the baroque style of writing is motivated by some formal development and linked to its moralistic intention. Although a first reading of the book carries one along, a second reading judges less convincing its originality.

Translated by Nicole Matiation

Notes

Originally published as 'La Proie des flammes', *Les Temps Modernes* 193 (1962): 1928–37. The French translation of Styron's novel *Set This House on Fire*, *La Proie des flammes*, was published by Gallimard in 1962. Another Styron novel to which Baudrillard refers, *Lie Down in Darkness*, was published in translation as *Un Lit des ténèbres* by Editions Mondiales in 1953. *Set This House on Fire* is available as a Vintage Reprint (1993; orig. 1960), as is *Lie Down in Darkness* (Vintage Reprint 1992; orig. 1951).

The two epigraphs to which Baudrillard refers at the beginning of this review are from *Lie Down in Darkness*. The first is from Joyce's *Finnegan's Wake*: 'Carry me along, taddy, like you done through the toy fair'. The second is from Sir Thomas Browne's *Urn Burial*: 'And since death must be the *Lucina* of life, and even Pagans could doubt, whether this to live were to die; since our longest sun sets at right descencions, and makes but winter arches, and therefore cannot be long before we lie down in darkness, and have our light in ashes; since the brother of death daily haunts us with dying mementos, and time that grows old in itself, bids us hope no long duration; – diuturnity is a dream and folly of expectation'. A lengthy epigraph from John Donne, extracted from 'To the Earle of the Carlile, and his Company, at Sion', opens *Set This House on Fire* and includes this passage: 'that that God, who, when he could not get into me, by standing, and knocking, by his ordinary meanes of entring, by this Word, his mercies, hath applied his judgements, and shaked the house, this body, with agues and palsies, and set this house on fire...'.

1. In the same manner, in *Lie Down in Darkness* alcohol plays a role of incestuous trickery. There is a whole analysis of the role alcohol plays in Styron's writing. He doesn't actually study alcoholism, although his characters drink from one end of the book to the other. For this look to Zola. Here alcohol is a sign, as epilepsy is in Dostoevsky, of the vocation of guilt. Alcohol hides and intensifies some desperate consciences, it is a sign of moral destruction, its power is multiplied by its link to desired humiliation, to the game of shame: it is a luxury, the wealthy drink. Illuminating the subjectivity, perceiving all situations through a sort of unfocused empty violence, it is the direct form of an alienated and uninhibited society, overwrought by leisure but especially pharaisic and puritanical to the highest degree. Once a collective celebration, here alcohol, like sexuality, is opposed to all the missed celebrations of this society which was industrialized too quickly, a sign of the absence of a sense of belonging that is felt as sin.

2. An odd character, quite artificial: why a fascist policeman who is very wise and sententious? And who obtains the confession from the murderer and helps him save his soul? I think that in this role that is absolutely that of the priest, Styron, in order not to shift the direction of the novel, chose to use not a priest but the most opposite of characters available to him.

Germany

Is It a New World?

One speaks of the Anglo-Saxon 'mentality', of the Latin 'genius', but of the German 'spirit', in the same sense as the Slavic 'spirit', or the Black 'soul'. For example: the Latin culture has a sense, the German 'spirit' has a destiny, etc. It seems that in people's mythology, this spirit has devolved onto private collectivities of unity, liberty, structured society, and historical responsibility. It is often connected to musical expression, and it stops with the actual political evolution of a nation.

We say that a people has a spirit when in some way it cries over itself, as the Germans have done over the centuries. Also, this spirit is very close to an imperialism without limits. Nowhere has this inconsistency gone so far as it has in Germany over two centuries, at the cost of the Germans themselves. For 'spirit' is a concept of inferiority and suffering, but when romantic, Wagnerian, Bismarckian, racist Germans begin to believe in it, it becomes a triumphal ideology of predestination. One who speaks of a spirit apparently wishes first of all to save that of others: 'The German spirit will cure the world!'

It has had its moment. Its weapons led its mythology to its end. Everyone tried to enclose it and take pleasure in it, the French with a sweet vanity, the Germans with a metaphysical fright before its image. The Great Reich was the fruit of this complaisancy. All of the peoples were dupes, but the way in which the Germans were dupes of themselves was the most dangerous for the others. However, it did not have fatal results.

That Germany has expressed itself over three centuries stage by stage through religion, music, philosophy, the will to power, racism, or more recently the transcendence of comfort – all tentatively leading to the end and almost always returning to the isolation of the world – we do not speak of the German spirit, or of those thousand and one Faustian Germanic spirits – that is too easy – we speak of those thousand princes or leaders who have set it on and led to its defeat. We say that, in history, the Germans have never found the thread, the freedom, the natural means of evolution that makes of a people. History has never succeeded for the Germans, this is a fact. An unhappy childhood, no political adolescence, a series of entries into great nostalgias (through the German myths and passing through the Holy Roman Empire up to the vital space of the present), of all this the Germans have kept up a problematic of accomplishment, of overcoming, a moving form linked to a great efficiency. A country of the middle and without measure, one could accurately wager that it will be the last one on this planet to find its equilibrium and unity. Goethe took his position on this, saying that it was necessary to transplant and disperse the Germans like the Jews throughout the entire world so that all the nations could profit from and have the best of them.

The greatest Germans have judged Germany from the depths of their exile – moral or not: Goethe from Weimar; Hölderlin from Greece; Heine from Paris; Nietzsche from Genoa or Nice; Marx and Freud from London, where they were in exile; or, in London again, during the war, where Thomas Mann sat in judgement over his people. Up to now, when a German is confused with Germany, it is for the worse.

Today, when contemporary history passes on its diagonal in Germany's direction, we do not speak in terms of 'spirit', no longer situating the Germans within this irrational complex. We are trying to understand the moment when they have detached themselves from it, in order to rediscover it, like the rest of the world, in their refrigerator. Things have changed. There are undoubtedly as many differences between the Federal Republic of Germany and that of William II as there are between it and that of Madame de Staël; the Holy Roman Empire, Luther, Bismarck, the bourgeois sorcery of blood and race are far away. Goethe and Hölderlin as well. Only Hitler is apparently close. But romanticism is no more.

Today, we have the immanent miracle of the imperialism of well-being. Everyone for himself and long live the German mark! Germany is far from the immense field of potatoes that Morgenthau wanted to make of it after the war. Not only have all its villages come back to life, but the Germans are building in the Indies, in Egypt, and Brazil. We should not be too hard: for the first time in fifty years, they eat away their hunger, and even more than their hunger, and this is fortunate for the rest of the world. But we should be fair: this is not truly an evolution.

In 1945, the Germans found themselves confronting a fundamental problem: how to erase their war-guilt, their total defeat, considering that it was a historical moment when they found all of the people against them. Such a guilt does not expiate itself: these are the old ideas of a twisted redemption, equally false at the level of peoples as they are at that of the individual. It does not resolve itself – least of all in analysing its causes: this has never been done. It transcends itself: in money, profit, consumption. Production and consumption have raised the level of ambition and destruction as a proof of the historical existence of a destroyed people. There is something in the effervescence of the German miracle, a special tone of exoneration, something like the transcendence of a fault in well-being, growth, practical efficiency. And the world understands this language. Herein lies undoubtedly a part of the certain affinity between Germany and the United States.

This Germany is fragile. At Cologne, at Hamburg, amidst the glass, the marble, and the leather, fifteen years later, there still floats a fading odour of carbonized cities. The churches sing, the factories smoke, everyone produces, everyone shops, there are no bottoms to the drawers in Germany: and yet civilization here is still quite problematic.

Possibly around 70 per cent of the population is happy, or satisfied. This is quite probable. The statistics say so. But the photographs that follow[1] do not take account of this satisfaction, and this is not by chance. What they reveal is something without a perspective on itself, something without charm. It is a satisfaction by default. One of the great problems for the Germans is still to ask what part Berlin plays in all this – Berlin is an imaginary capital, Jerusalem glowing and encircled – their greatest cities have the universal character of London, Paris, or Rome (and with the cities, the press, fashion, luxury, culture …). And they are not so sure of it. Through the standing of their cities, there is always the nostalgia of a universal credit that troubles the Germans in the middle of their wealth.

There remains Berlin. 'A city that would serve as a rallying-point would be very useful to Germany', said Madame de Staël in 1810. Today Berlin has truly become the German capital. Unfortunately not in the harmonious sense of Paris or London, but like an abscess of fixation. The strange similarity between West Berlin and West Germany reflects the entire federal mentality: a curious mixture of euphoric justification for its standing and the morose enjoyment of the victims of communism. From the image of Berlin, the Republic wants to make itself rich and menacing: this is its entire ideology. An unhappy sign of the impasse of this federal mentality is the decay of culture.

Before one has spoken of 1945 as the Year O, one may ask oneself seventeen years later: Is Germany a new world? As the will to power, at the middle of the last century, had placed it step by step on the path to cultural aspiration, so this time the economic adventure has taken up the race, with an indestructible dynamism one never sees anymore except in Germany or the virgin colonized territories. But is it actually an adventure? Is Germany in the process of change along the lines of a brutal Americanization? Will it ultimately lose its 'spirit' and find a style, or, by a stroke of chance, create a new society? It hardly seems so: in Germany today, one speaks in terms not of a society, but of a community. And everything, in its absolute modernity, still has this provincial, hierarchical, and patriarchal character, the source of those many perilous virtues, and over which floats 'Europe' like the pious wish of the West.

The East, for itself, is dedicated to a true collectivity. There, too, for the moment, there is only one wish, not more pious, but equally brutal. However, the constraint here has a definite goal: social organization. It lacks charm, but it is a perspective. In the West, growth is without end. What will emerge from this confrontation? At any rate, we do not minimize the experience for which, after so many others, Germany in its totality is currently the theatre.

Every developed, urban, technical civilization, especially if it is 'miraculous', gives the impression of unreality. In the Federal Republic of Germany, this impression of unreality is a little more ponderous than elsewhere. It would be difficult to say exactly why – but certainly also by the refusal to envisage this precise situation: there are two Germanies, and, year by year, the people's conscience follows a different path, on one side or the other of the Wall.

Translated by Peter Flaherty

Notes

This excerpt was originally published as a preface of sorts under the title of 'L'Allemagne est-elle un Nouveau Monde?' in René Burri, *Les Allemands, Textes réunis et présentés par Jean Baudrillard*, Paris: Robert Delpire, 1963, pp. 6–12.

1. *Trans. Note.* The photographs of René Burri constituting his study *The Germans*.

Review of Uwe Johnson's *The Border*

Toward the Seventh Spring
of the German Democratic Republic

In a small Mecklenburg town on the seashore, a man and his daughter: Cresspahl and Gesine. It's 1945. A mother and her son, Jakob, arrive with a convoy of refugees. The children grow up as brother and sister under the same roof. While Jakob becomes the dispatcher in a large railway yard along the banks of the Elbe, Gesine heads to the West and becomes an interpreter at NATO headquarters, a nice prize for the secret service in the East, who would be happy to bring down this dove on the roof. After an initial contact with her adoptive mother, the latter flees in horror to the West. Jakob remains. He is a secure man, a capable technician, an upright citizen, and pillar of the handball team. Power has cast its eyes on him. Herr Rohlfs contacts him. Jakob does not accept his offer, but promises his silence, since he does not want his socialism to go any further than his work. Suddenly Gesine crosses the border, arriving in the East at the time of the Budapest insurrection. In the course of a tumultuous flight from the border guards, fraternal love becomes love pure and simple (this is not the crux of the action). They arrive at the father's house in Jericho, where they also meet Jonas, assistant professor in East Berlin, an oppositional intellectual caught up in the movement of the XXth Congress. He, too, loves Gesine, having met her in the West. All of these people, whom the border has crossed either ideologically or practically, meet for a long night of discussion with Herr Rohlfs, an official in the regime and leader of the game. The regime itself is at stake in Jakob's decision, but this decision does not take place. Gesine returns to the West. Jakob finds her again shortly thereafter, under the ever-vigilant protection of Herr Rohlfs, but the border and the division of Germany are stronger than personal motives. The West is not acceptable to Jakob. He returns, and on the morning of his return he is hit by a locomotive on the very tracks 'that he crossed every day' to get to work. We are left to make speculations about his death, as the German title reminds us, *Mutmaßungen über Jakob* (*Speculations about Jakob*).

The book is an autopsy. Jakob is dead before the first line, and the opening sentence raises an objection to his death. How could someone who always used to cut across these railway tracks have been crushed in this way? The question recurs right up to the end of the book, opening on to all possible interpretations. Johnson is cunning: through nuances he knows how to trigger an unverifiable hypothesis (we never know if Gesine herself is a secret agent of NATO – there is only the presumption), but he is not bluffing. He wants to recover and describe Jakob, a significant person of the GDR and thereby globally. In opposition to Rohlfs, the bureaucrat who seems to think that an individual can adequately be explained by his or her biography, 'as if the stupid sadness of a pot of flowers on the windowsill in a room stripped of all furniture was a faithful description', Johnson has Jakob himself say that the circumstances of someone's life have nothing to do with the person. By contrast, all these words describe qualities, and this man seems to have none. In any case, he must have no qualities. Johnson's own method transpires across this dull, insoluble presence, consisting as it does in recalling techniques, causes, and conjectures and in representing all this as necessary.

Since his death is without meaning, that is, since it is only an end, Jakob cannot be analysed, explained, or justified; he can only be described as dead. Because appearances may only be artificially coordinated when their relation to the person is indecipherable, deeds and gestures remain as so many multiple versions of Jakob. In this way, the chronology of the dialogue and monologue become entangled, taking this death as their point of departure by reversing the scheme of the detective novel where everything converges on the resolution of a single death.

This is because Johnson is not a sentimental detective, but a philologist:

> Philology deciphers and explains unknown words by taking up clearer citations from other written documents; it compares dictionaries, grammars, regional maps, archaeological discoveries, the flora and fauna of the imprinted countryside. It gropes about to recover the syntax, the system by which sentences are formed; each dialect has its own special dictionary with a grammatical appendix. Among the different versions of a text, it searches for the one that seems the most correct (the least deformed) etc.

This is Johnson's method as transcribed by Jonas. It is neither psychological, nor ideological, nor historical. There are no political 'lines' or reflexive motives that together seem forced, that give gestures a distracting splendour, and that thereby disturb the description. A speculation sustains the appearances, and Johnson wants a speculative description of Jakob's life (or death). This is the same method used by the descriptive sciences, and entails two complementary requirements: speculate on nothing beyond the faces, gestures, and functioning of things, but forget none of the details. Something concretely important, serious, new, and minute is imposed in the course of deciphering the world. This method is not a battle of wits, and it guesses at nothing. It is a method of scientific reporting, and it is the same as Jakob's method of dispatching. Basically Johnson himself plays the role of dispatcher by making his book run on multiple tracks that serve as multiple versions and different modes of the narrative. In spite of this confused density, we know that somewhere a dispatcher is watching over the punctuality of the book. This is why it is not humorous.

If he was to follow his inclinations, Johnson would undoubtedly add more notes, commentaries, and variations to the already complex polygraphy of the text. This is because he belongs to the race of Jonas and Karsches: decipherers, bewildered commentators, meticulous researchers who are at the limits of their intellectual abilities, philologists in exile, *Aussenstehender* on the margins, whose only resort is to apply their rigorous (but perhaps also outdated) science to a new object – political man. Precisely in terms of its object, this method might be criticized, and in particular we shall see that it is applied more to the description of objects than to men. Johnson is the first to admit failure. He might be reproached that his human motives are hardly convincing, that his books have no soul, that they are inanimate, dry, and insensitive. Certainly he establishes an unsurpassable distance between himself and his objects or the characters of his narrative, avoiding the interior world and keeping only its outer dimensions. But he also guards against romantic epilepsy, that is, the painful identification with his own characters and literary sublimation. When they fail, he himself fails to give an account of their defeat. Like Jakob, he finally realizes 'at what point he is irreconcilable'. The romantic sign of this irreconciliation is Jakob's death, which signifies nothing else. Worse would be to reconcile oneself with this death through a psychological or ideological solution. Thus Johnson is content to leave this death with the whole of its questionable value, removing all its dark poetry.

'I haven't conducted any experiments concerning the mood of the narrative. I have waited to know and grasp the necessary form for the story that I knew and wanted to tell'. But what does Johnson tell? The border. 'The characters are imaginary, events do not refer to similar events but to the border, to difference, to distance, and to the attempt to describe them'. This is the inscription that heads the second of Johnson's novels, *The Third Book about Achim*, which begins by invoking the iron curtain. In fact it involves the character of Karsch the journalist, but he and his appearance and the motives behind his trip are less important than this break in the road with its elementary suddenness, this ending of all paths before a wall, an embankment, a ditch. Apart from any calculated style, this is what is Faulknerian in Johnson: all his stories and their vicissitudes are rooted (often remotely) in a discord, in the almost metaphysical rupture between the two Germanies, as in Faulkner between Whites and Blacks. Johnson deserves praise for not making this rupture metaphysical, though it becomes so when one does not have (and does not want to have) an ideological view.

This basic situation confronts us on all sides: the smallest gesture is not only a perilous sign toward other people, but passes above an objective, geographical, and police border without surmounting it. And this seriousness is not just the shadow cast by the story as it gives rise to heroic effects, but the irreparable fault, the distance that one senses like the atmosphere of all things:

> I take up this theme [of division and reunification] everyday with my breakfast, without having to read the newspaper. This state of things has transformed the lives of many, and my own in a primordial and sometimes negative way. We shall find a solution for it or it will be our loss.

This poses a new problematic for description. Either we are in the East or we are not. There is a choice. A tree may even be a tree beyond the border. Each thing must be described for its political exigency.

All meanings are tangential to the border, and this is said on each page not as an element of suspense, but as the meaning or viewpoint of the book which all descriptions envelope. From this emerges the slowness of the narrative, its terminological prudence, the meandering (however consciously) of its thread. Somewhere Johnson says that it is not the eyes that give a face expression but what surrounds them in flesh, eyebrows, and moving muscles. Thus he seeks to encircle the secret of a new and fundamental break with the details of Jakob's life, of the life of man. This is not the rupture between Good and Evil, between Black and White, but the political one between East and West for which Jakob's death is the expression. And whether one wants it to or not, this border crosses us all.[1]

Nevertheless this central thesis is still poorly posed in the first novel, since Jonas has bungled his role: his dismissal from the Institute, his relations to Gesine, his arrest at the end, are hardly convincing and remain in Jakob's shadow. The anticipated East–West confrontation does not take place, and the one between Jakob and Rohlfs is lost in theoretical discussions.

There is no desired 'difference' as it suddenly appears in the second novel, and so no analytical design or desire for a much clearer objectivity. Reading *The Third Book about Achim* makes *The Border* (that is, *Speculations about Jakob*) appear as a rather romantic essay, an atmospheric book with mystifying effects,[2] fleeting motives, slack periods, and useless twists and turns. A certain number of influences can still be perceived and the whole leaves the impression of a more or less conscious compromise between the style of the period and personal style. In *Achim*, Johnson renews the experiment on the same basis, with the same characters and further along the lines of a critical literature.

It tells the story of Karsch, a Western journalist who leaves for the East to see his friend Karin, an actress. Karin is now living with Achim, a bicycle courier who is the darling of the masses and deputy in the People's Chamber, and so enjoying the political favours of power. The Western Karsch is fascinated by this anomaly, this new type of social hero, and resolves to describe him in a biography. But where is Achim's truth? Once this ideological truth of the State is isolated (of which Achim is both an employee and a symbol), Karsch is disarmed. He is left with the old psychological conundrum of inventing deeds and causes where there are none, of animating, exalting, and romanticizing to make good literature. But the figure of Achim resists, and Karsch goes to all this trouble for nothing. All of these traditional literary false starts of intuitive poeticization and showy reappearances, that is, this whole context of a naïve and cunning imagination that is part of the usual romantic approach, is described at the beginning. The book is a critique of literary probability understood as parallel to a critique of experiential probability. Through Karsch, Johnson surpasses what is entailed in the illustrative novel with its formal truth in order to approach the didactic novel more closely. He has given his novel a subtitle: 'Description of a Description', indicating that he wanted to get beyond the step of a realistic critical method in literature.

Karsch comes directly from the West and the entire Western intelligence apparatus. He finds in Achim a kind of strange normality, that of the man of the East, which he then proceeds to analyse. When he fails, he leaves, and the border momentarily suspended by this encounter once again descends. But this border, which Jakob sensed somewhat as a constant disturbance, has become a fact worthy of science (but always tending towards failure). People and things are cut out in space. A clear method (each chapter begins with an exacting interrogation) is transported by a confident language, contained by a rhythm or played out through rhythm and its suspension. This surprising science of language is often linked for whole pages with Goethe's classical descriptive objectivity in *Wilhelm Meister* and *Elective Affinities* (an iambic verse is even used in the description of armour). Of course this verbal research technique cannot be separated from language considered as an instrument. On the one side, there is in Johnson a danger of a cold and limitless virtuosity, of jargon. On the other, there is the danger that hovers over all didactic novels of using stereotyped objectifying language: the diction of the apparatus, indirect style, language which is participial and bureaucratically formal, gerunds, russified Saxon, in short, 'a whole senile syntax', 'the kachoube conspiracy', in the words of Hermann Kesten. Though more detectible in *Jakob* than in *Achim*, this does not compromise the method. It is a defect.

If we began by speaking about method and the border, it is because Johnson himself starts from difference and the method for describing it. But behind difference there are naturally different men, those of the East. They interest Johnson because they are born in difference and carry the (problematical) chance of a different society. Jakob is not a profound hero; he is clear and yet indescribable. Stripped of images of himself (since only in the West, where Gesine lives, are there mirrors and photographs) and with no interior monologue (as he never speaks to himself), only the monologues and dialogues of others allude to him. He becomes visible from various social angles – that of Cresspahl (the peasant artisan), of Rohlfs (the Secret Service), of the dispatcher (technical responsibility) – but these are not 'circumstances', and Jakob does not hide behind his actions. He is rather something like a political man, even if he is far from knowing this and only glimpses it. In Achim's case, this is already quite clear. The level of political participation is different in the two novels, but each concerns a man 'whom the State loves and who loves the State'. This new relationship becomes fundamental in the human situation itself.

The mother is absent, lost. In *The Border (Speculations about Jakob)*, she goes to the West at the beginning of the book and reappears at the end only in photos. As Jakob remarks, 'it is like she's dead'. Achim's mother disappears in a bombardment and is not to be found, leaving only her dresses behind. Is there some deep motive in Johnson's own life that explains this absence of the mother? In any case, this disappearance orients the book toward the extreme of a regular familial structure: the intensification of brother–sister relations (eventually becoming incestuous), the renewal of relations with the father, and especially the progressive transference of oedipal relations to an adoptive father – Rohlfs in the first novel, Fleisg in the second. Behind these two characters is the State, which 'has cast its eyes on Jakob'. Rohlfs, an important figure in the Secret Service, directs what might be called the book's detective dimension: taking on the suspiciousness and individual constraint of the socialist State, he is the *eminence grise*. Nothing about Jakob escapes him, except Jakob's death, which also escapes the others, and he himself hardly exists apart from Jakob. Complicity, shadowing, theoretical discussions that suddenly become familiar – all are part of the murderous Rohlfs with his past as a fighter for socialism and frustrated father, who loves Jakob like a son, both as his personal hope and as the chance of society. This tenderness is nevertheless clearly in service of the regime. It can even be said that here in a society where all familial structures are lost, Rohlfs translates the universal aim of the State (its defeat as well) by substituting himself for the Father – as simultaneously guardian and enemy, protector and judge. But for him social reason is matched with an affective fixation. Undoubtedly he has a purely political relationship with the State, since for anyone born after the seizure of power the State has made you what you are (negatively in the case of Jakob, positively in the case of Achim), and everyone is tied to it through recognition: such is the affective component of today's socialism (which is different for revolutionary solidarity). The Rohlfs–Jakob relationship allows us a look into this society with its slow progressive collusion of the human and the political. Having no real mother or father, and between one adoptive father (Gesine's, his adoptive sister and lover) and another (Rohlfs, his political tutor), Jakob's familial space has disappeared. Politics increasingly takes its place, and Jakob finds himself alone in the midst of severely altered relationships in which oedipal feelings curiously mix with the new requirements of the State's political collectivity. Is this an unsolvable disturbance? Jakob's death in the mists of the very railway yard where he worked, the site of his own social praxis, is itself unsolvable (is it a suicide, a fatal accident, has he been liquidated, and if so why?). There is no sense of destiny in the book, nor is there the murkiness of a detective mystery. Beyond any useless interpretation, his death is a sign of man's real inability to adapt to real means of action, of the lack of equivalence between this new society and the man it requires. This is the sense in which this death is a judgement on the GDR. Under the appearance of political equilibrium, Achim's analysis also reveals the same contradictions. The border is not just between East and West, as it does not yet appear to have been lifted between the citizen and man.

In the two novels, woman is the contradictory sign of this double border. It is Gesine who brings together and then separates Rohlfs and Jakob, while Karin questions Achim's relation to the State by calling Karsch to the East (later we discover that he participated in the riots of June 1953). Likewise, in both cases the woman is tied to the man from the West by having lived with him for a time. Between the two, however, she never provides the dramatic element. In Johnson love involves rather a kind of profound solidarity which is at once definite and knows no tomorrows; it is thereby stripped of all subjective representation. As lively, vibrant, ironic, and distant figures, neither Gesine nor Karin participates in the stakes of passion. They have the clarity and the freedom to be judges and witnesses, and in a way that is also rather Goethean; they sensitively reveal the problematic of the book: their personal choice (between Jonas and Jakob, Karsch and Achim) is itself determined by a historical line of division. When in the end the border once again descends, they find themselves alone.

Johnson's characters are definitely part of the classical tradition. If we think of the bourgeois novel from Goethe to Thomas Mann in which this exceptional individuality (by birth or by cleverness) mediates society, we can see very well what has changed: through their work (dispatching or cycling) the figures of Jakob and Achim are representative. We are indeed in the East, but we are also not far from the classical novel, insofar as dispatching and cycling cannot be described either realistically or mythologically as a 'milieu' like the railway or sport. Rather, as in *Wilhelm Meister* and *Faustus*, they are conveyed through a *typical* description and by way of a *typical* figure who comes from a society in which a human type takes form through new mediations. Such mediations are no longer a kind of free bourgeois intellectuality, but are part of the materiality of labour, technology, and social relations.

Johnson's novels would be socialist in this sense if they were in the least tied to a proletarian class consciousness. But they are not and cannot be so. Jakob and Achim are officials and in no way proletarian. They mediate the fundamental problem in this society between the people and the State. Their problematic is that of socialist man after taking power (while all of Brecht is situated before). What language can describe and what concept can (perhaps) subsume this new man? What are his life chances? Here, too, Johnson seeks no reconciliation, nor is he falsely impartial. By interrogating the human condition, he starts from the requirements and objectivity of description. Through the eyes of Jonas or Karsch we see a bit of this Political Man as a strange and new species.

Somewhat like Goethe, Johnson describes for us the original plant, the *Urpflanze*, with the same concern for finding the organic law (rather than the secret) of a new system: namely, the transition between a lived subjectivity and an assumed collectivity. He loved the State and the State loved him. What would come of it? Karsch tries to retrace the individual progress of this being through infancy, adolescence, Achim's loves, and a million hypotheses until arriving at its typical, social, and collective meaning. In the same way, Goethe tries to recover the harmonious genesis of the entire vegetable world through the spiralling of leaves. What is at stake in both is the universality of modern man and his need to be political. This perspective is undoubtedly not very socialist in the dialectical sense of history, but today the socialist description of socialist man is not to be found. No one yet is able to pass through the divergence that lays the foundation for such a man or the border that crosses him. The level of descriptive and critical science only allows for hypotheses about him, about his defeat (Jakob) or his relative success (Achim). Only ideology comes before the solutions, though not for Johnson. Only description is situated at the level of the knowledge that can reasonably be expected of a confused global situation which is characterized by the coexistence and confrontation of the two blocs and which is full of all kinds of resolutions that will determine the world of the future. But who can say? In the limbo of the border, only a tireless curiosity, though limited in its means, has any validity. This is why, even without future perspectives (and without humour), Johnson's novels are not dark. Is he personally counting on a protracted social praxis or on the evolution of deeds? Even in his interviews he is not very talkative about this. 'If politics can be understood as an art of living, then I am interested in politics'. He is not a manager of conscience but only an artisan of language suited to articulating problems: if Karsch fails to describe Achim, the critical foundations laid by Johnson in the description of this description will allow others one day to go further.

Johnson's method attains its goal in the description of things. Human worlds are still impenetrable and strange to one another. A practical description of them is impossible since their praxis is not exact. Consciousnesses confront one another, their history is murky, and History is not in sight. Only things which are structured are animated and can truly animate the narrative. Johnson is not interested in the dead or haunted objects of the 'objective' novel, in objects that become inhuman agents and witnesses for the prosecution by having been meticulously described. Rather, his concern is with living and functional complexes which have social uses, such as the switch-point, the mechanism of a bicycle, the sporting event or the typewriter, which for him are the perceptible form that the collectivity takes in the life of everyone.

In Johnson this always begins with terminology. The organization of things begins with the disorganization of the lexicon, that is, with a need to scatter accepted concepts. Thus he calls a camera 'the carrying case of memory' (this is a limiting example), since what is subsumed in a word, whether communism or a camera, is false. Whatever side we are on, our way of naming things is already ideological. If we want to understand Achim himself, we must decompose such things again into their simplest elements, to redescribe the bicycle in the primitive mode of the natural sciences as 'a metal apparatus with two wheels in which movement is effected by etc.'. And if we want to grasp in depth how a collectivity reasons, we have to describe in minute detail how people walk or cross the street, no longer calling things by their name but returning to their practical description. In a world where the lexicon itself has become a catechism, this would amount to a radical critique. Johnson will go so far as to ask: 'What would it mean to transfer the control of large enterprises to the workers?'

Hence the methodological desire to describe railway dispatching, workout sessions, or ideological conversations. One could call it *Akribie* (a German term for a German quality, namely, meticulousness or a fanaticism for detail). But there is nothing in common between, on the one hand, the ice cube that slowly melts in a glass of whisky or the fly circling around a light, the formal object and nothing, and, on the other, Johnson's felicitous, totalizing descriptions of collective objects. In these descriptions there is almost a tenderness, a freshness of discovery which is devoid of any pathetic belief in technical progress. Man has simply cancelled his metaphysical contract and made another more perilous and collective one with things. Once accepted, the technical character of the world almost becomes natural and simple again, a secure basis for transforming not just things, but men. This is socialist, but not socialist realism! It is not the sentimental vision of collective work, the pathos of the tractor and the gas stove in which the reconciliation of man and the world is already hypocritically celebrated. Rather, it is an open materialism attached to the orientation of things and of complexes of things, but which does not presume upon their meaning. Here, too, Johnson is not interested in political ends. Technology is *klassenindifferent*, that is, neutral with respect to class. In place of the ideological meaning of history, Johnson would put the actuality of praxis and of functional use, without apology or romanticism – the world of Praxis, rationality, and objectivity. Meanwhile, freedom is conjectural: it is either too late or too soon for freedom.

In a sense, the perspective of such a science (since it is indeed a scientific perspective) is nevertheless political and social (but let us not take this further than

Johnson does). The moment from which one can only ride a bicycle rationally, crouching for the sprint in the most effective way possible, constitutes an adequate element for the social generalization of socialism (given the sense of responsibility and moral integrity of a man like Achim or Jakob). The same goes for dispatching trains or the map of a city. Practice is extolled, that is, the devotion to a social object that can compensate human alienation at the political level, or perhaps even absorb it. In contrast to disputes between humans, the description of things has an optimistic and joyous tone (especially for Achim). Tired of a personal god but eager to be saved, the pantheists found the god of the heavens in the grass and stones. Tired of socialism's historical determinism or the State's dogmatism, though still vehemently desiring rationality and solidarity, Johnson has lodged his socialism in objects and their uses. This constitutes a kind of artisan's Marxism, with its heated rationality, devotion to detail, and mistrust of supreme agents. Jakob and Johnson have no history, nor do they want any. Having accepted socialism, Nazism (which has harshly caught up with Rohlfs) hardly touches them. They are not revolutionaries, but concerned instead with the everyday practice of transformation and adjustment. This is today's problem with socialist man, and our own as well. Johnson is indicative of this modern problem: man's exact recognition as a function of his technical capabilities for action on the world. This may or may not be carried out politically. For his part, Johnson refuses to give it an ideological turn. Is this a limitation? Certainly not in literature.

'Literature communicates to us the relationship that a determined subject has with the world. From the point of view of the sciences of mind, what linguistic means did the eighteenth century use to conquer and dominate the world?' Johnson's design for literature is to apply the same spirit of steady patience and varied investigation that Jakob applies in his work as a dispatcher in the organization of things. In this sense, the same dignity based on the same method is suited to philology, dispatching, cycling, or novelistic description: the laws of praxis are the same in all these areas, and thereby provide the elements of a socialist practice. If literature must change, it must become a concrete tool which is constantly critical and demonstrative. At least in the case of Achim, we are not far from Goethe or Brecht. At the level of the problems that concern us, literature has never been closer to a concrete science, to the search for its object. However political they may be, these books are immensely important historically since they do not just confront the organic problem of the division of Germany; they also clarify the whole situation of the citizen of the East and our own situation at the crucial historical moment of the crisis of the XXth Congress, and thus an entire epoch of peaceful coexistence and its contradictions. They do not tell us about the distressed modern 'individual' with his allergic reaction to other people. They speak to us about the man whose emergence is also that of his political consciousness. In their intractable concern to reevaluate man's practical and political possibilities, these novels became possible only after 1953. They are not *engagés*. Through their use of objective description, they are living proof of the degree to which the political determines us and in what respect we are conscious of how it determines us.

Translated by Thomas Kemple

Notes

Originally published as 'Uwe Johnson: La Frontière', *Les Temps Modernes* 199 (1962): 1094–1107. Uwe Johnson, *Mutmaßungen über Jakob*, translated into French with the title *La Frontière* [*The Border*], Paris: Gallimard, 1962 and into English by Ursule Molinaro as *Speculations about Jacob*, New York: Harcourt Brace, 1972; *Das dritte Buch über Achim* (Frankfurt: Suhrkamp), translated into English by Ursule Molinaro as *The Third Book about Achim*, London: Jonathan Cape, 1968. At the time of Baudrillard's review, *Das dritte Buch über Achim* was in the process of being translated into French.

1. In support of this thesis concerning borders and distances, note the importance in the book (symbolized by the two main characters) of the material means of communication (telephone, car, railway: Jakob) and of intellectual comprehension (languages, interpreting, philology: Jonas).

2. 'And until sunrise the sky was a leaden grey'. 'And the sky was white all day'. The wind, the rain, the sky, the grey light, the absence of colours: an atmosphere of limbo, of dullness, of a violent indistinctness, somewhat equivalent to the mist and the violent indistinctness of the North in Faulkner: this is the novel's Baltic atmosphere.

PART II
CRITIQUE OF MASS-MEDIATED LIFE

Review of Marshall McLuhan's
Understanding Media

We are entering the Electric Age which follows the Era of Typographic Literarity (Age of Literacy). An era of 'explosion' followed by an era of 'implosion'. The Electric Age puts an end to many centuries of visual culture, of technical specialization, of individualism and nationalism, and reintroduces instantaneous communication and the tribal relation (which once were those of the oral cultures preceding printing). Such is the *generic thesis* of this book.

McLuhan has written a general 'history' of civilizations from the perspective of the evolutionary process – based not, as with Marx, on techniques and forces of production, but on techniques of communication: the media. This formal history is based on a *binary typology*: 'hot' and 'cool' media, articulating three great 'historical' phases: tribal cultures – cool; literacy – hot; Electric Age – cool. All this is founded on a *theory of signification* which is summarized in the formula: 'THE MEDIUM IS THE MESSAGE'.

Every ten years American socio-culturology produces great leading schemata or synoptic analyses of all civilizations which take contemporary American reality as implicit goal and model future. One finds here again the great threefold schema of the 'lonely crowd' which is that of all mythic thought. Sorokin, Toynbee, Riesman, McLuhan, and others: great nominalist prophets, categorial thought (the media function here exactly as the great moral, economic and cultural categories of the 'classic' systems), curiously mingled, however, with pragmatic observation, often well founded, and with a cultural impressionism often rich in insights, which makes these great books intellectually shocking and irritating, a stimulating read.

What is 'literacy'? Inaugurated by the movable type of Gutenberg, it is typographic technology, based on the phonetic alphabet, on blocks (*découpage*) and visualization. In rationalizing all the procedures of communication according to the principles of continuity, uniformity, and repeatability, it overthrows the tribal organization of oral structures of communication. Fundamental *medium*, therefore true *message* of the West, this model has inserted itself little by little into production and the market, law, science, education, urban organization, and culture.

Across reading and writing (technically mediated) it is this same revolution which is taking place in the countries of the Third World, initiating a process of standardization which leads to the visual organization of time and space. McLuhan reports the fright and utter astonishment of indigenous people on discovering the simultaneous existence of *many* identical books: without the technical cutting-up of the world, of the field of perception and interior experience even in a homogeneous space, there would be no modern civilization, no economic 'lift-off'. Now the absolute model of this technical division, therefore the medium of this first great 'historic' revolution, is 'literalized' discourse, technically materialized in space it is the printed book – homogeneous succession of lines of letters, in pages, in books, collections, libraries, archives, etc. – with the ultimate phantasy of a world responsible for this 'literal' organization, and therefore susceptible to a total 'reading'.[1] All the oral structures, tribal and feudal, are swept away: 'The giving to man of an eye for an ear by phonetic literacy is, socially and politically, probably the most radical explosion that can occur in any social structure' (McLuhan 1964: 58).

We are still living with the consequences of that revolution. But today, with the total medium which is electricity, we are inaugurating a second (and ultimate?) global revolution, after that of Gutenberg. Whereas the former media were only mechanical and visual extensions of the body or of work, electricity (electronics, cybernetics, etc.) is an extension of the central nervous system.[2] Whereas the traditional schemata born from 'literacy' used to imply mechanization, specialization, inductive causality, the technical division of labour, great central organization, industrial and imperialist 'explosion', electrical instantaneous non-visual communication changes everything. Even causality: one passes from linear connection to configuration. Everything at once becomes contemporary and decencentralized, a process of planetary synthesis installs itself ('implosion'); no more continuous, homogeneous, abstract space – each configuration creates its own space-time (here modern physics rejoins the perception of the archaic, non-'literal' cultures): 'Feedback is the end of the lineality that came into the Western world with the alphabet and the continuous forms of Euclidean space' (McLuhan 1964: 307).

Paradoxically, with this fluid network and unlimited interdependence, our civilization finds once more, beyond the 'Age of Literacy', the schemes of intense participation and inclusion belonging to the oral and tribal cultures. Automation (and already the telegraph, the TV, etc.), far from being an extension of the mechanistic principles of division, of succession and of exclusion, is the sign of a regrouping of the planet through 'instant' and generalized communication. Satellites and electricity bring back the entire planet, beyond the bygone reign of the towns (typical phenomenon of the Age of Literacy), to those organic structures of the village (which had institutionalized human functions on the basis of intense participation and weak organization; formula for stability); we are thus returning to a synthetic and tactile world (in McLuhanesque terms: iconic and mosaic) of implosion, of equilibrium and stasis. The irony of this synchrony is that at the same time we rational and visual Westerners, beings of 'literacy', are having as much difficulty (McLuhan speaks of 'moral panic') on entering into this new universe of configuration, supple and tactile, inaugurated by electricity, as the indigenous people of the Third World on leaving their oral and tactile culture in order to enter 'our' universe.[3]

In contrast to so much (above all European) mass-mediology, with its generally morose futurology, McLuhan is perfectly optimistic. The sombre narcissistic vision of the media as metaphorical autoamputation of man changes with him into an 'immense collective surgery' (still tactile values). 'In the electric age we wear all mankind as our skin' (1964: 56); the electric age will create in the world one single collective consciousness, etc. 'Panic about automation as a threat of uniformity on a world scale is the projection into the future of mechanical standardization and specialism, which are now past' (1964: 311).

This optimism has an evidently simple basis: it is founded on McLuhan's total misrecognition of history, and more precisely the social history of the media. That said, his periodization of the great technological eras of media is not any more absurd than any other. He has after all indexed the great truths often badly formulated in cultural terms in a quite baroque new cybernetic lexicon. It is here that he becomes difficult to follow, especially where he distinguishes between 'hot' and 'cool' media, on which he bases all his speculation. 'HOT' are the media which, in principle, deliver the most information (high definition), and require the least participation and 'empathy'; the 'COOL' media are low in information (low definition) and are the media which demand close contact, where one plays the game (the best example of 'cool' would be betting, which fascinates because it is poor and formal in its corpus of rules).[4] All the oral tribal cultures (pre- 'literate') were 'cool', based on rites, dance, symbolic gestures. All the literate cultures (books, science) are 'hot' because they rest on distance, non-participation, the faculty of disconnecting action and reaction. Therefore the book is 'hot' (it is this which can appear paradoxical), but also the radio, the cinema (this is less paradoxical), which are for McLuhan prolongations of the book in the electric age (this we do not understand very well).[5] Today, with television (and the cartoon, strip cartoons, advertising), we are entering into a new 'cool' era.

This we do not understand at all. The schema of McLuhan is logical in terms of his thesis, but illogical and ambiguous in reality. Indeed, which participation is it about? Affective investment, empathy, passive fascination, 'addiction' (TV)? Or active participation, intellectual or contemplative (books, work of art)? Certainly works of op art, or kinetic art (both typically 'cool'), are regarded with more curiosity, more fascination, than anything by Vermeer. But what does that signify? What is curiosity?

Let us come now to the most impassioned and perilous paradox of the book: 'The Medium is the Message'. In this cybernetic form it is somewhat equivalent to the Marxian formula: 'Feudal society is the windmill ...'. The virtue of such reductive formulas (as false as one another taken literally) should not be overlooked. McLuhan means the book-medium (but this would be even more true of current mass-media) has transformed our civilization not so much through its content (ideology, information, science), as by *the fundamental constraint of systematization which it exercises across its technical essence.* He means – and it is true that here consciousness is always veiled – that the book is first of all a technical object, and that its ruling organization is more pregnant, more determinant in the long term, than any symbol or information, idea or phantasy which it carries. 'The effects of technology do not occur at the level of opinions or concepts, but alter sense ratios or patterns of perception steadily and without any resistance' (McLuhan 1964: 33).

This is evident: the content hides for the most part the real function of the medium. It passes for the real message itself whereas the real message, of which the real meaning is perhaps only a connotation, is the structural change (of scales, models, *habitus*) which operates in depth on human relations. Roughly speaking: the 'message' of the railway is not the coal or passengers it carries but a vision of the world, a new status of agglomerations, etc. The 'message' of TV is not in the images transmitted, it is the new modes of relation and perception that it imposes, and which change the traditional structures of the family. More generally still, in the case of TV: what is received, consumed, assimilated – its real message – is very much less this or that show than the virtuality of the succession of all possible shows. That is the TV-object, the TV-medium: its precise result (if not function) is to neutralize the lived, unique eventful character of that which it transmits, to turn it into a discontinuous 'message', a sign which is juxtasposable among others in the abstract dimension of TV programmes.[6]

It is by the technological support that each 'message' is in the first place transitive towards another 'message', and not towards a human reality. The TV images of Vietnam send us much more towards advertising than towards the war. At the same time – according to McLuhan's idea – the medium makes us bounce towards other media. The cinema draws in literature, literature into language. The photo draws in painting; today, painting integrates the photo. The TV is, firstly, an object – specific medium – but it transmits images – another medium (which can draw in other objects: in Africa, for example, the indigenous people are sensitive not to what goes on TV, but to the décor of Western objects, of which the representation is subversive in the tribal and underdeveloped context – whereas for us the TV is an object, not perceived as such, transmitting images, for them they are images [often not perceived as such, wondering what happens to characters who leave the screen] transmitting the objects).

In brief, a multiple universe of media homogeneous to one another is constituted signifying one to the other and drawing one towards the other – reciprocal content of one to the other: at a push this is their message – the totalitarian message of a consumer society.

The silent film called for sound, said Eisenstein. The black and white cried out for colour. All objects call out for automatism (not those who call, but in the use, evidently). It's as if there was a *process of technological inertia*. This process of technical perfecting of the media goes against the objective 'message' of real information, of meaning: the Vietnam war in colour and in relief only brings out the real absence of the war. Yet the technological process delivers well, however, a certain sort, very imperative sort, of message: the message of the consumption of the message, of spectacularization, of autonomization and potentializing information into a commodity, the exaltation of the content as sign (in that sense advertising is the contemporary medium *par excellence*).

Other media can cease being the 'means' of such autonomization as the very substance of the message: language, of which the usage is often less transitive towards a praxis than 'culinary', borrowing a term from Brecht, consumed in its heavy materiality of signs. The group: it is also a medium which tends to constitute itself as a message, independently of all content or objective purposes, etc. 'The Medium is the Message' is therefore a paradox which one can push quite far in order to expel ideologies of content. Generalized, it would be the very formula of alienation in technological society. Systematized, it is also the best way to evacuate sociology and history. It is this which is its weakness, or the ruse of McLuhan. If one admits, with Georges Friedmann, that the message always ends by putting one man face to face with another, one must admit also that there is never a cultural dictatorship of the message (or of the medium) as such, and that beyond the fundamental determination that it exercises, a concrete analysis must recognize the relation which must pass between men or between groups (sociological analysis) – and on the other hand the mode of production of the media, and on their structures of power which come to articulate this production (historical and political analysis). McLuhan does not bother with these subtleties.

Once more, if his vision is so resolutely optimistic, it is because his formation rests on a technological idealism which makes him disregard as anachronistic, behind the 'infrastructural' revolutions of media, all the remarkable historical convulsions, ideologies, the persistence (and even the recrudescence), of political imperialisms, nationalisms, bureaucratic feudalisms, etc., in an era of 'communication and accelerated participation'. If the modern media are the extension of the central nervous system, the individual and group find means of investing, at the same time as their unlimited informational possibilities, their power structures and their regressive phantasms. McLuhan does not speak of these matters. His book is fragile and brilliant. It lacks, very simply, the historical and social dimension which would turn it into something other than a mythological 'travel shot' of cultures and their destiny.

Translated by Mike Gane

Notes

Originally published as 'Marshall MacLuhan, *Understanding Media*', *L'Homme et la Société* 5 (1967): 227–30. All references in the text are to McLuhan's *Understanding Media*, New York: McGraw-Hill, 1964.

1. It is a question here not of a 'structural' reading, of grasping the world as syntax, but of a technical decoding of the world as phonetic alphabet, of an apprehension of the world, not in its significations, but in its materiality of discourse, writing, the fabricated object-book: the discontinuous succession of an irreversible order of signs called letters.

2. Let us cite in passing the curious psycho-mythic reference of McLuhan to Narcissus/narkosis in order to produce a genetic theory of the media = extensions of man. Organic extensions (voice, gestures, language, clothing, housing), techniques (books, machines, etc.), nerves (radio, TV, electricity), light being the total medium – all these media are metaphorical projections of man (as the image of Narcissus) and at the same time are 'autoamputations' by which man searches to reestablish a menaced interior equilibrium, to conjure away tensions in technology, which interpose themselves as his own

image (and, as with Narcissus at the origin of the myth, alienated and non-recognized), between him and the world.

3. McLuhan reproaches Marx for having based all his analysis on a medium – the machine – already superseded in his time by the telegraph, and other 'implosive' forms. Already the 'mechanical' dynamic was overturned by a new problematic that Marx had not seen and which rendered his analysis null.

4. Significantly one finds here once more the oppositional couple 'hot/cold', of which Riesman made one of his major criteria of the 'other-directed' personality.

5. An absolutely fascinating idea: the most violent effects result from short-circuits between 'hot' and 'cool' – for example the brutal introduction of the radio, a hot medium, in a cool culture: oral and indigenous. According to McLuhan's logic: the irruption of the TV, a cool medium in our literary and traditionally scientific (hot) culture, of which we are far from having understood all the consequences.

6. Same thing for indigenous people flabbergasted when faced with many identical books: it is that very seriality which puts an end to their charismatic universe where the message is always unique, bonded to the messenger. Thus with printing: it is as techno-logical support that it puts an end to feudal structures, much more than its humanist and Renaissance content, which comes later and represents in fact very little within the volume of printed writings.

Technique as Social Practice

All technical practice is social practice, all technicist practice is immersed in social determination. But such practice does not present itself in this way, claiming instead to be autonomous, innocent, claiming to be Technical Reason, grounded in Science. Such rationality underpins the ideology of Growth, which imposes itself on our society as if it were a moral code, and is where technicist practice, cut off from the social Reason for which it exists, becomes a technique *of the social* – or, more precisely, a technique of social manipulation, and therefore a technique of Power. The practical efficiency of Technique is transformed into social effectiveness. But this is too general a statement.[1]

It would be interesting to see how, in every era, the technical possibilities are taken into the logic of privilege. In the fifteenth and sixteenth centuries, those at the top of society kept the most advanced techniques to themselves, and used them for their celebrations. Over time, but most noticeably in the twentieth century, the most advanced techniques become those of the military, and the military is strictly in the hands of Power. The ruling classes generally only let filter down what is absolutely necessary for the reproduction of the productive forces. They even go so far as to wilfully organize stagnation or technical shortcomings. Technique, and the uses made of it, has forever separated the social into distinct areas, categories, and zones of privilege. Discrimination through technique is a given throughout history.

However, it is only when technique emerges completely from religious, ritual, ludic, and corporative constraints, and when, along with the Industrial Revolution, it becomes a free productive force, that it elevates itself into the totalitarian myth of modern societies. This is still too simple, as it is not the effect on society as a whole of something overarching called 'technique' that we need to analyse. What we need to look at is how a society becomes stratified as a result of technique; what links the various classes or groups have with each other through technique as practice and as myth; what social strategy comes into being from that, and what sort of relation exists between social discrimination in the context of a value system called Technique, and social discrimination as it occurs in other value systems, such as Culture.

The myth would have it that whereas Culture is the site of hereditary inequality, Technique would constitute a 'democratic' dimension. According to this myth, individuals from any social background would be more naturally and spontaneously equal when it comes to Technique than they are with regard to Culture and Art (and there is even an inverse privilege attached to the underprivileged classes, being closer, as it is said, to the empirical world and the mechanical arts).

According to this myth, Technique would be a field that is more rational and, as a result, more democratic, as virtually anyone can get into it, through a process of training and practice, as opposed to the subtler paths into Culture and Political Science. According to this myth, Technique would be an entirely innocent field, separate from politics. It would be innocent as it is to do with the mastery of Nature, whilst Culture, Economics, and Politics would be more directly involved in the organization and mastery of the social.

Against this myth, Technique is only an instrument for the mastery of nature and the freeing up of productive forces right at the beginning, or at an initial level. It is, at the same time, an instrument for restructuring social relations and for the development of a social rationality. Once it has gone beyond a particular level in the mastery of natural forces (and for us, this threshold has long been crossed), Technique becomes first and foremost an instrument of mastery and of social control. And this occurs in two ways: directly, as an adjunct of Politics, and indirectly, as a mechanism of acculturation.

The political dimension: with all social imperatives being subordinated to those of growth, and therefore to the controlled use of technology, the mastery of the conditions of technological research and the singular control of the higher technological operations (particularly military research) creates, for Power, a radically new privilege, upon which base the whole game of politics is played out. All investments and economic movements depend for their existence on this monopoly. The way in which secret rituals and the tools of the Sacred were possessed was never, in any period, in any society, as exclusive as the secrecy and technological manipulation by the State in our modern societies. We would of course have to investigate sociologically the structures of this monopoly, defining techno-political decision-making groups as opposed to there being pure technicians, on the one hand, and traditional politicians, on the other. We would also define the particular technicist ideology of such groups, as opposed to the technicist myths for the use of all, and so on.

The cultural dimension: Technique, far from unifying society on the basis of knowledge, actually acts as a form of discrimination between levels that is as certain, if not as traditionally and hereditarily based, as that of any cultural initiation. This system, like the other, works through institutions dedicated to technique, and a system of Technical Education as inferior vocation. The former (e.g. Research Institutes, The Science Academy, the National Centre for Social Research [CNRS], secret space and atomic research centres) sanction, at the highest level, Technique as a model and as a universal value. At this level, Technique is sublimated into Research and Science. Technical Education, particularly in our Western societies (even if we might wonder whether praise of technical values in the East is not fundamentally linked to economic objectives), remains ambiguous in its double, and shameful, link to the teaching of Culture and to theoretical scientific teaching.

The marked inequalities that this mechanism establishes in the real involvement in technical knowledge tend to be hidden by the diffuse mythology surrounding Technique. This hierarchy – official or officious – is subject to a very powerful social code. Between theoretical and vulgar practice, between a noble technical knowledge and applied knowledge, or, still lower, between the application of simple technical operating instructions and do-it-yourself, between access to treatises on nuclear physics and reading contemporary science or an instruction book on domestic techniques, there is a whole sliding scale of status, one that is regressive. Each one of these indicators reveals a particular social state, and comes together with others to assign each group its appropriate rank.

We need to be clear about this: it is about status, and not about knowledge. It is not about concrete differences in knowledge, which, logically speaking, have nothing to do with social hierarchy between people. It is about social *distinction*, class distinction based on the *quality* of knowledge taken as an indicator of *value*, and therefore of a *genuinely cultural system*. It is about a code of social designation that no longer works through a literary or artistic *habitus*, but through a lower or higher degree of *initiation* into the technical order.

In the social logic of culture, technical order, as a system, comes into play, and this, with relation to the system based on humanist values, as a parallel *system of acculturation* replacing the former and filling in (with very similar mechanisms) where the traditional system of acculturation would break down.

Technique constitutes one of the most powerful themes in mass culture. Within the population there are substantial social groups, essentially untouched by the genuinely cultural versions of culture, that are only capable of being integrated through the dreams, impulses, and fragmentary bits of knowledge given out in the field of technique.

The widespread phenomenon of autodidacticism – the standard process of catching up engaged in by the middle classes as they emerge as such – feeds, to a large extent, on technique. All those who are left by the wayside by scientific or cultural training attain their salvation, one way or another, through Technique. It is not that they have a natural inclination towards it. Rather it is the logic of the overall cultural system which assigns them to this subculture, which lives off the prestige of science, in unconscious resignation.

On top of the direct power that it confers through its political efficiency, Technique brings a parallel, ideological power that it acquires from the fact that it functions as a pseudo-culture. It is a secondary culture, destined, for the main part, for the uncultured classes, but is still a systematized culture, with its apparatus, its points of legitimacy, its mechanisms of transmission, its models and its norms – it functions, in short, like a total cultural system that comes to reinforce the other, so as to confirm the hierarchy of powers within society.[2]

So, we will only be able to capture the ambiguity of Technique if we analyse the position accorded it in the framework of an overall value system: rendered sacred as the ultimate means of power in the arena of international economics, technique is still an ignominious educational and cultural value. We also need to analyse how is it that our societies fail to autonomize technical values as worthwhile in their own right, and come to transcend this failure (or rationalize it) in a universalist myth of Technique.[3]

But, basically, if our societies do fail to rationalize technique as social practice (and not just as technical practice), this failure is precisely not an innocent one, for to rationalize the practice of technique would be equivalent to giving up the mystery of technique as a basis for social practice.

In a hierarchical society, technique, like many other things, is not supposed to be there to function, but to provide the *mystery* of function. And this mystery, which lays upon every technical product, every point technique occurs in the social body, is a social mystery.

The Organization, as Myth, of Technique

Technique presents itself first and foremost in social terms – once outside the abstract and rational mode of pure technology – as a double system, one of systematic opposition between two terms where each justifies the other, with these two terms being: a Metatechnique, and an everyday practice. One is a transcendent Technique, brought into being in fiction, and the other is technique rendered mundane, reified as part of consumption.

This distortion of technique is often talked about in terms of spin-offs. Everyday life, maintained in a state of technical infantilism (for strategic reasons), benefits nonetheless from the spin-offs of high-level technique. This presumes an acceptance of the argument that there is uneven development of the different sectors within social life, and behind this is the hypothesis that there is a theoretical unity, a transparency within technique, the glorious spread of which is curtailed only by social structures.

In reality there is no technique other than that developed by people in given social contexts, and no meaning of technique apart from that which it acquires within social logic. This social logic, however, establishes technique from the outset as a bipolar ideological system. Far from it being a case of social organization coming along to separate a unitary technique from its true principle, it is the social, and it alone, which installs technique, and installs it as something divided up, discontinuous. It is the social which gives technique (in its status of social signifier) this logical distance between two poles as its basis.

Sublime technique, banal technique. Fiction, everydayness. Between the two, no great distance, nor any 'spin-offs'; rather, a logical distance and a contradictory mutual involvement. In this, Technique is homologous to Culture – both follow the same social logic. Furthermore, there is no Highbrow Culture which would have Mass Culture as its 'spin-off' (in terms of individual versus mass-produced item). There is, from the very beginning, an entire cultural system based on the logical distance between Highbrow and Mass Culture, with one defining itself in terms of the other, with each implying and also excluding the other. This to the benefit of Highbrow Culture, which is the guardian of the definitive models.

In the same way it can be seen that Higher Technique, *in its very progress*, has as its base the principle of the dividing up, through technique, of everyday life, and also the giving over of the latter to the stereotypes of consumption. So it is not at all an accident of society if everyday life is in a state of chronic technical under-development. This is far from being a malfunction, as it is a function that obeys the *logic* of the system, just as a certain amount of poverty and hardship is a functional element of the 'welfare state'.[4]

It is in this tactical doubling that the imaginary comes into play. Higher Technique, cut off as it is from daily technical practice and muddled up with Science, can come to serve as the imaginary of the banal technique of consumption, just as Highbrow Culture basically serves as the imaginary, in terms of being the standard, for Mass Culture. The worship of technique that comes from nuclear and space research, from futurism – all of this creation of new worlds, all this science fiction – can come into play through domestic gadgets, which, as a result, are not experienced as spin-offs, but are transfigured as signs and promise of a total Technical Revolution, the model for which is already there. This is hinted at throughout the wild and euphoric discourse on Technique (and this discourse always comes complete with a pessimistic moral discourse, which only serves to heighten the sense of intoxication). The average individual thinks themself a total citizen of the Technical Revolution, through the panel of their washing machine, but this panel, with its caricatural power, coming from an archaic world of functions, is in fact not doing anything at all except consigning them to the absence of any complete, innovative, or restructuring technique, and this in turn is consumed as absence. In this way, the most insignificant of everyday objects implies the total functionality of a completed world of technique, beyond any social contradictions, beyond history. This is the other element of the social mystery mentioned earlier.

Technique, then, comes about in major, mythical, oppositions, such as that between rocket and car. In practice, the opposition between a technique seen as prestigious and one that is obsolete is no more than apparent. A whole civilization is clogged up in the concrete dictatorship of the car, and the fascination with the adventures of the space programme. These are the two poles of a systemic contradiction within which both technique and everyday life surround and are alienated one from another.

As a result of this systemic doubling, where one term works as the imaginary of the other, technical objects do not come directly into everyday life as mediators of new social functions and structures, but rather are *already mediated by the Idea of Technique*, and by a metaphysics of rationality.

This signifies, in concrete terms, that new objects and techniques are not lived as practical and social innovations, but as a sort of intermittent novelty, acquiring their fascination from their complicity with the Myth, the Future, the imaginary, and not at all from any possibility they might have of changing the present. This is how they come to be received as OBJECTS, that is, fixed and idealized as avant-garde SIGNS, populating an unreal everydayness. This is how they fall into CONSUMPTION. And this with the following paradox: the more technically new they are, the more they are seen as aesthetic and destined for consumption by the wealthy.

So this is how Technique, which is immersed in everyday life, comes to be realized as science fiction, feeding an aesthetic of fascination and simulation, giving over all its power to the prestige to be had in consumption. The same thing happens, more or less, to any technical object or set of procedures, as happened to the filmmaker, as Edgar Morin showed convincingly in *Le Cinéma ou l'homme imaginaire (Cinema and Imaginary Man)*: the immense possibilities for information, communication, and social change opened up at the beginning, in terms of a scientific technique of the image, fell away almost totally, and seemingly irrevocably, into the imaginary – leading to Cinema as Spectacle, and the Cinema of consumption.

Conclusion: 'Technique Totally in the Service of Everyday Life?'

If one allows that Technique presents itself, at the outset, and within the social logic of class, as just such a system described above, and therefore as a system of mythical transfiguration of real contradictions (those of everyday life and of social structures), then what about the revolutionary slogan that is Lefebvre's 'Technique Totally in the Service of Everyday Life?'[5] In practice, for technique to bring about a revolution in everyday life, there would have to already have been a revolution of the whole system so as to make Technique something other than it is.

The hope of revolution is based on the premise that there is a fundamental rationality to the technical order that only needs to be freed and articulated through social reality in order to overturn it. But it is not that simple. Such a rational level of technique certainly does exist – in the form of technology. But whether as private individuals or as social subjects, we do not have anything to do with technology. What we have is technique in the form of a system of values and ideology. So what hope is there if Technique is the product (of the most efficient type) of the very social order the failure and contradictions of which are masked by Technique's rapid progress, thus taking away the possibilities of their resolution? How can we hope to put Technique in the service of a social revolution?

Up to a point, to do so would be to make the same mistake that lies in the claim that 'the police would come to be totally in the service of the collectivity', when, by definition, the police is social, and serves private interests and Power. The same could be said of Culture.

In short, we should avoid thinking of the technical dereliction of society as an accident that happened on the way, and that all we need do is to put technique back on the track, free up its potential, and life would be changed. We need to see that it is our society, itself, at its deepest level of organization, that reinvents Technique at every passing moment – as a dimension not of knowledge, but of salvation; as a mythical system and power strategy, as opposed to a rational instrumentality and revolutionary social practice.

In any case, there is no possibility of any revolutionary 'irruption' of technique in concrete society. In order for technical innovation to bring about real structural changes, there has first to be installed a *technical culture* – and that through the slow and difficult substitution of traditional culture by another value system. This would occur through a *whole, radically different, educational system*, different not so much in its content, but in its training *techniques*. We need to finally get out from the Technique of the Spectacle of Technique, and the myth that surrounds it, so that we recognize it through the principle of its functioning (which is that of 'capability and rational usage'),[6] and transport this principle right to the root of social training, if we want to really get rid of all the magic trickery.

Translated by Paul Hegarty

Notes

Originally published as 'La Pratique Sociale de la Technique', *Utopie* 2/3 (1969): 147–55.

1. *Trans. note.* The word 'technique' in French approaches the sense 'technology' now has in English. I have kept 'technique' as it implies process and procedure and, as will be clear later in the essay, is to be distinguished from technology. For this reason, 'technique' in the original should not be deemed to have been simply the contemporary word for technology.

2. The socialist countries have encouraged the high valuation of a technical culture. However, it seems that after a while (in Hungary and Yugoslavia), the hierarchy of traditional values, briefly overturned, tends to return, to the benefit of cultural values. In any case, profound changes in the cultural *habitus* can only come about in the long term.

3. *Trans. note.* Here, the original text directs the reader to the footnote that appeared at the end of the previous paragraph.

4. *Trans. note.* English in the original.

5. None of this excludes the *real* changes that technique brings about each day in everyday life or in social relations. These are undeniable, and considerable, only these changes work *inside a system* whose function is precisely that of controlling the evolution of the system, and making sure that the changes never establish any overt contradiction.

6. Strictly speaking, this principle has nothing to do with actually existing sciences or techniques. We need to remove 'Technique' from its use as an absolute category, to return it to its concrete efficiency, where it is always technique OF something – of rational training and usage.

Review of Henri Lefebvre's *Taking a Position: Against the Technocrats*

In this book, Lefebvre sets out to attack systematization, systems, and System alike (the capital letter here, as with Brecht's masks, is to expose the absolutism of a concept that is both mystified and a mystifying one). With such a view, this could hardly be a straightforwardly earnest book without in turn mystifying the reader, and as we see, it has brilliance, humour, spontaneity, and *appassionato*. It is more – and better – than the tract some were waiting to see. It is a living example, in its very writing, of the antisystematic.

Having said that, what it addresses is not a laughing matter. Technique, instead of producing a social rationality, has become misleadingly mixed up with ideas of Progress and Happiness (more capitals, sadly), and is well placed to replace any and all living social practice and to constitute itself as a total political ideology in the hands of the technocrats. The idea of Revolution has been transferred, now referring to the drastic development of technique that supposedly occurs on a daily basis. A mythical system develops wherein the contradiction between the rocket and the outmoded car is only an apparent one. The very concrete dictatorship of the car, within which a whole civilization gets clogged up, and the abstract fascination with the adventures of the space programme are, in practice, two poles of a huge systematic opposition within which both technique and everyday life surround and are alienated one from another. So everywhere, in production and consumption alike, we see the development of closed systems, closures, structures dedicated solely to their internal coherence, all given over to computation and rational calculation. The cybernetic model of closure, control, and servocontrol has infiltrated everything (and in fact all this is the cybernetic myth, as the most advanced technology is challenging it today). It is in human organizations as much as in technique, in human sciences as in mathematical sets.

This is a crucial point, as not only does social political practice get invaded by a metalanguage of organizations, within which the sense of contradiction in social relations disappears from lived experience, from works, but analysis itself organizes its approach on the basis of a systematic vision. It is structuralism that has everywhere taken over from a faltering dialectic, and that claims to account for the real through the play of signifiers alone, through a *logic* of manipulating signs, which is itself also a *strategy* of the combinatory type. Structuralists and technocrats are both involved in the arbitrary manipulation of signs and institutions (behind one and the same language of rigour). Lefebvre categorizes this structuralism as a new Eleaticism, opposing the Marxist dialectic of history, as Zeno and the Eleatics, theorists of identity, balance and stasis, once opposed

Heraclitean becoming. For Lefebvre, structuralism is no longer happy with just denying that history can be scientific; it now disputes the fundamental nature of historicity as conceived by Marx, in regarding it as an ideology past its sell-by date; it oscillates between rushing back into archaeology (to societies previously called 'primitive', to the unconscious), and hurtling forward into what is yet to come. Its aim is to sideline lived experience in order to attain the real, and its seeking of structures becomes bound up with immutable laws. Its model is linguistics, where the structural enquiry was an influential innovation.

Lefebvre is far from disputing the use of any such method (Marx was already speaking in terms of structures), but he does wish to dispute the theoretical generalization that leads to a metaphysics of the System, to the normative extending of structurality to all levels, to the logical (almost ontological) preexistence of structure, which implies a timeless validity for the structuralist model. Through this, he is questioning the metalinguistic abstraction of structural discourse, which allows itself – through an epistemological separation from the empirical real, and through the rigorousness of its closure and of its game of relations and oppositions – the scientific illusion not only of organizing facts and finding laws from them, but also of avoiding the traps of history and the exhaustion/integration in advance of all possibilities. In practice, Lefebvre argues that the arrival of structuralism is historically relative, and its discourse is not one *on* our society, but a discourse *of* it, and one that, in taking itself to be a metalanguage (science), is no more than connotation (ideology).

This, basically, is the central argument of the book, along with the opposition between the invasive metalinguistic function and the evanescent referential function. In other words, the message is more and more to do with the code, and everything is just writing on writing. There is no real interpretation of the world, as instead we have internal redundancy, rhetoric, pleonasm, connotation. So it is that all signs and every discourse end up looking no further than themselves, congratulating themselves on their coherence. At this point, some further comment is required.

In the first place, Lefebvre himself, in the course of his forceful critique, does have a tendency to give a pejorative connotation to the notion of metalanguage, in a way that is overly systematic, on occasion mixing it up with straightforward rhetoric, as in the metalanguage of the Revolution, alongside the metalanguage of commodities (advertising), and so on. If some metalanguages (and certainly not all) are merely redundant, despite the epistemological separation, they are redundant in a way that is more subtle, and, in whatever logic you are following, radically different from connotations in rhetoric – Lévi-Strauss's metalanguage is not that of Godard.

Second, theorists of structure do not claim an immortality for their approach. Barthes, in *The Fashion System*, says that structuralism knows itself to be a mortal language, reducible (but to what?). It is about not a *historical* relativity, but at best an epistemological one. No evolution of history will come to supersede the structural approach, as it relativizes itself totally, through a structural process of reduction *en abyme*, without ever in the process starting up a dialectic. The alternative to this is still therefore radical.

Finally, can we infer, as Lefebvre does, daringly (in tracing a line through the Eleatics to Lévi-Strauss, to the technocrats and to American imperialism), from the logic, or the wager, of structuralism that it colludes with the System and the existing order? In other words, does analyzing reality in terms of systems amount objectively to bringing about a systematic reality? It was not enough that Marx analyzed history in dialectical terms for history to have taken the dialectic path of the Revolution. So here we have a major epistemological problem: is a dialectical reality (the class struggle) subject to justification by dialectic thought; is a structured reality, or one in the process of systematization, subject to justification by a structural(ist) or systematizing approach, such that when taken to its logical conclusion (by Lévi-Strauss), thought on myth can only itself be a mythical architecture (see *Mythologiques*)? If there is a system in the real, how can we account for it, if not by a systematic analysis? The critique of Systems as such, undertaken by Lefebvre in *ideological* terms, can be based only on a *logical* analysis of their processes and their set of functions. In order to expose false rigour, the antisystem must be totally rigorous, and turn the System's own weapons on itself.

Having said that, it is clear that all thought of system has a tendency to become systematic, that is, to constitute itself as the sole meaning of its own discourse (i.e. having formal coherence), and even, through this, as the perfect expression of a tautology of Power. And this through an ethics of suggestion and auto-production, which should also be analyzed structurally. In its very perfection, in its obsession with closure, the thought of systems becomes the utopian sanctioning of an order that it only decodes in order to complete.

In order to check the (technocratic) System in terms of social practice, Lefebvre opposes the institution with the work. This is a something newly produced, a *poiesis*, a revived everydayness, for which all the resources of technique can come into play. To check the thought of systems (i.e. structuralism), he offers two types of response, or perhaps it would be better to say that he hesitates between two types of response which do not really come together, apart from in the polemic drive of the book. These types being:

First, an analysis of levels. So in language there would be a phonological level, a morphological and lexical level, and a translinguistic level (phrase and story). This last level comes not from the structure, but from a situation (even if today there is a move to the structural analysis of story). This level would move beyond, moving toward lived discourse. Such a move is the opposite of, and in some way corrects, the previous epistemological separation. Elsewhere, in his analysis of the world of suburbia, Lefebvre brings to light the existence of three different levels: lived experience/functional; mythical/structural; political (i.e. power). The first two combine into a system of denotation and connotation, while the third is history. However, is it possible to give the levels a dialectical relation in order to maintain, in an overall perspective, the benefits of structural analysis?

The notion of levels seems to me too empirical, and all that it implies in terms of its analogy with liquid dynamics – difference in level, tension, balance, moving through (and not moving beyond) – renders it too weak to make the two approaches (structural and historical–dialectical) function together.

Second, Lefebvre has occasion to take a different perspective in order to reject structuralism, one that is clearly dialectical, Gurvitchian. This approach is interested in structuration over structure, subsystems, destructured and restructured subsections, different temporalities, gaps (linguistic and social), that which cannot be put into structures, and so on. He sets up a radical opposition between the open totality, the order which can contain all possibilities, and the human element that cannot be destroyed by the closure of the System or its tautological order. His statement that which can be systematized is that which is already dead summarizes pretty clearly, with its echoes of Bergson, this alternative outcome.

Is there something illogical in having these two versions? I don't think so, as the 'position' is one, and it is against, whilst its propositions are many. The expression of the dialectic conveys the vigorous refusal of the very nature of structuralism's approach, and the device of using levels is a way to strategically manage the methodological aspect. Is it a genuine strategy?

Once more, the overall notion does not seem to me to be enough in itself to make the weapons of structuralism work against it. In any case, the attraction of the book, its diversity and freedom all add up, in their own right, to a demonstration that efficiently attacks the System.

Cybernanthropes,[1] sadly, will probably read it with pleasure!

Translated by Paul Hegarty

Notes

Originally published as 'Henri Lefebvre, *Position: contre les technocrates'*, *Cahiers internationaux de sociologie* XLIV (1968): 176–8. The book under review was published the previous year (1967) by Gonthier.

1. *Trans. note.* Lefebvre's term, referring to those who would seek to make us and our surroundings more cybernetic, more systematic, more technocratic.

Ephemeral and Durable

The ephemeral is without doubt the truth of the future habitat. Mobile, variable, and retractable structures fit into the formal demands of architects and the social and economic demands of modernity. But this is only true in an ideal dimension. One must not lose sight that:

1. Neither the ephemeral nor the durable is an absolute and exclusive value. Only their constant relation and the multiple play of oppositions between them found a logic of cultural significations. One can reorient their relationship and bend it according to social rhythms: in this sense, everything really pushes us toward an accelerated mortality of objects and structures. Nevertheless, the two terms only have meaning relative one to the other.

More precisely: if clothes, objects, appliances, and the car comply more and more with the norms of the ephemeral (but there is a limit), nothing says that they are not all together against 'inhabiting' it – this constituting a specific function which could be brutally or ideally assimilated to other aspects of consumption and fashion. The symbolic design of these is allocation and expense; the symbolic design of inhabiting is that of foundation and investment. To reduce the two to the same ephemeral synchrony is without doubt to liquidate an entire field of very rich contrasts. Yet there is lived culture (just as logic of sense) only in the tension between these two poles.

2. It is true that today there is a colossal social deficit that represents the fragmentary or whole construction as hard and durable: it contradicts economic rationality and social exchanges, the irreversible tendency toward greater social mobility, and flexibility of infrastructures. However, the latent psychological, familial, and collective functions of the 'hard' and the solid need to be taken into account – these are very powerful functions of integration that include them in the social 'budget'.

3. Some day, the ephemeral will perhaps be the collective solution, but for the time being, it is the monopoly of a privileged few whose economic and cultural standing permits them to call into question the myth of the durable.

It is because bourgeois generations have been able to enjoy the permanent and secular setting of property that some among them can today give themselves the luxury of renouncing stone houses and exalting the ephemeral: this custom belongs to them. All the generations of lower classes, by contrast, whose past opportunities for gaining access to the cultural models and to durable property were non-existent – to what does one want them to aspire, except to live the bourgeois model, build castles for themselves and their children, a derisory dynasty in stone residences or suburban housing tracts? How can one 'promote' for these classes today that they not regard property as sacred and agree right away to the ideality of mobile structures? They are doomed to desire things that last, and this longing only expresses the cultural destiny of their class.

Reciprocally, the cult of the ephemeral implies ideologically the privilege of the avant-garde: according to the eternal logic of cultural distinction, a privileged few savour the instantaneousness and mobility of architectural structures at the moment where the others just barely rise to the quadrature of their walls. Only the privileged classes are entitled to this year's models. The others are entitled to them once they have already changed.

If, therefore, in the logic of forms, the 'ephemeral' represents the truth of modernity, perhaps even the future formula of a rational and harmonious society, it still acquires an entirely different meaning in the present cultural system: if, in its foundational logic, culture plays continually on two *distinct* terms (ephemeral and durable), neither of which can be autonomized, in the socio-cultural system of class, this relation splits into two *distinctive* poles, from which the one – the ephemeral – autonomizes itself as a superior cultural model, relegating the other to 'obsolescence'.

This is not at all to disqualify the formal research of architects; but there is bitter derision in the fact that this research into social rationality precisely ends up reinforcing the irrational logic and strategy of the cultural system of class.

Translated by Timothy Dylan Wood

Note

Originally published as a marginal note in Jean Aubert's 'Devenir suranné', *Utopie* 1 (mai 1967): 95–6.

Dialectical Utopia

We want to situate ourselves in the uncrossed interval which exists between theory and praxis. Praxis (conservative) situates itself in the existing order. Grasp the urban totality and all its contradictions; apprehend all possibilities. Social possibilities are present and to be made – in the sense of coming into being; the urban contains and confines them; it is essentially a matter of freeing them and bringing into play their revolutionary potential.

This existing order is a *topos*. Its critique and analysis enable one to elaborate the *utopia*; define, situate and critique it, and update the means for its realization (philosophical, political, economic ...).

UTOPIA has two fields of possible realization:

1. The existing power, whatever it is, assimilates the means, critiques, and projects of the *utopia*, and therefore, in a certain measure, its goals, by rejecting it. But, even if there hasn't been some fundamental modification of the existing order, a part of the *utopia* passes into reactionary praxis anyway.

2. The revolution which destroys the *topos* permits theoretically a total realization of the *utopia*, which then becomes a *topos* (revolutionary). One cannot determine in advance what will constitute the revolutionary praxis of the *topos* and what will remain theoretical and reintegrated in theory.

The realized *utopia* is a new *topos* which provokes a new critique, and then a new utopia. The installation of the utopia occurs through an urbanism (total). And this is the complete process.

Topos (conservative)–critique/utopia/revolution–urbanism/*topos* (revolutionary and conservative)/new utopia ...

We call this DIALECTICAL UTOPIA.

Utopia is the phase of theoretical construction, but it is absolutely indissociable from the other phases and cannot exist apart from the *dialectical utopia*. It is only by the *dialectical utopia* that we can elaborate, outside and within the current system, an urban thought.

Translated by Gary Genosko

Note

Originally published as an unsigned editorial statement under the title of 'Utopie dialectique', *Utopie* 1 (mai 1967): 54–5.

Utopia

The Smile of the Cheshire Cat

Utopia has been suspended in idealism by a century and a half of triumphant historical dialectical practice. Today it begins, in its rigorous indefiniteness, to supplant all revolutionary definitions and return all the models of the revolution to their bureaucratic idealism.

Utopia is the non-place, the radical deconstruction of all the places of politics. It affords no privilege to revolutionary politics.

There cannot be a model of utopia, nor a utopian function, because utopia repudiates the inscription of every finality, whether it is in the unconscious or class struggle.

Utopia is not only the denunciation of all the *simulacra* of the Revolution, it is also the analysis of Revolution as a political *simulation* model of a rational deadline for man which opposes itself to utopia's radicality.

Utopia is never spoken, never on the agenda, always repressed in the identity of political, historical, logical, dialectical orders. It also haunts and crosses them irrevocably, forcing them into an overstatement of their rationality. Utopia does not inscribe itself in the future. It is always, from now on, what the orders lack.

In the topics of the sign, utopia is this gap, this fault, this emptiness which passes between the signifier and signified and subverts all signs. Utopia passes between every thing and its model, annulling their respective places. It displaces politics without end, and in so doing annuls it.

Utopia is not the dialectic of the possible and the impossible. It is not what overcomes contradictions dialectically; rather, utopia transgresses them in their own terms.

Utopia is the ambivalence which crosses every order, every institution, all rationality – even the 'revolutionary' kind – all positivity, whatever it is, and flips them into their non-place. It is the deconstruction of every unilateral finality of man or history.

Utopia is the smile of the Cheshire cat, this smile which floats in the air before the cat appears, and for some time after it has disappeared; a little before the cat appears, and a little after it has disappeared. This smile into which the Cheshire cat disappears, and is itself mortal.

Utopia is that which, by the abolition of the blade and disappearance of the handle, gives the knife its *force de frappe*.

That our discourse analyses everyday life – celebrations, strikes, the media, and sexual liberation – and denounces everything in them which is subject to phantasms, slogans, and current revolutionary models and appeals, beyond the code, to the radicality of the symbolic and ambivalence – this contains a fundamental contradiction – worse than a contradiction: the insoluble position of all theoretical discourse which is irremediably rational, didactic, and political and whose speech subverts no part of the code of the analysis. Too bad. Before cancelling itself out in a more radical practice, something must be said.

Translated by Gary Genosko

Note

The original editorial statement had neither author nor title and appeared in *Utopie* 4 (octobre 1971): 3–4.

Police and Play

To say repression is to say CRS.[1] But this is a dangerous impressionism. The dramatic evidence of repression, when it suddenly appears on the surface of the cities in the uniform of the Special Brigades, only obscures the latent system of repression which haunts the depths of our consciences. One of the victories of the May movement was to have conjured up repression and caused it to surge forth as the truth of social order and institutions. However, its weakness was to have conjured it only in spectacular form, under its deadly and archaic aspects, upon which, to be sure, was founded a tactical solidarity (every one against repression), but upon which also the movement became exhausted in spectacular guerilla warfare, ending up in a fascination for symbolic street confrontations in which, in iconography as well as in the obsessional folklore inspired by the CRS, repression incarnate became the *number one object of consumption* for the imaginary in revolt.

If the May movement was caught in this trap, in this game, in this symbolic counter-dependence which forms part of our cultural mechanisms (which it nevertheless attempted to overtake towards the end by means of the slogans of enterprise self-management), we can admit that it was the tactical political conjuncture which brought this about, and that, over and above police violence, the movement targeted the fundamental social violence, the repressive instance of the political, the violence of every kind – sexual, cultural, economic – inflicted upon people by the social order *as order*.

But it is not enough to see this as a radical insurrection against society regarded as a carnivorous flower or the political and transpolitical reincarnation of the Bad Mother. Even if it is true that this kind of genetically remote phantasm, aimed at the subversion of the very principle of social reality, fed the contestation of global society, we must understand the specific mechanisms of repression in contemporary society in order to explain its resurgence. What new type of repression incites this new type of insurrection?

In order to understand repression we must abandon not only the police schema but also the empirical schema of the repression of vital forces, the frustration of essential needs, which has been vulgarized by psychoanalysis. In civilized countries, repression is no longer a negation or an aggression but an *ambience*. It is the pacified day-to-day in which there is no longer any distinction between police and play. In other words, generalized repression, which involves the internalization of contraries (intellectual and sexual) and in which the repressive instance becomes *maternal*, is the site of an intense *participation*. The era of overt co-repression is being installed behind the maternalist jargon of environment, ambience, incentive payments, and participatory values which has replaced the social lexicon of the

Word of the Father, the normative and judicial jargon of Order, Justice, and Hierarchy. This repression is imponderable since it operates by signs. It cannot be conjured up in the street or by street combat because it is inscribed in the very outline of the street, in the travelling shot of the shop windows and the spectacle of street combat. In the case of co-management, it is fed by the very signs (but only the signs) of responsibility and power. This historical transition from violent forms of repression towards complicit euphoria can be read in the face of the city: the Parisian *Grand Boulevards* which were formerly the sites of insurrection and violent repression have become great arteries of commerce and spectacle; social conflicts are no longer resolved there by force, they come there to be abolished.

This repression, which appears at the level of lived experience as complicity and *ambience*, takes in theory the opposite form of a total system of division and *separation*. Social violence today is expressed less by means of the direct repression of drives, the physical constraint of individuals or the overt oppression of a particular class or category, than by the imposition of a grid of social relations, by ever more complex and systematic geographic, professional and cultural segregation, by the irreversible technical and social division of labour and by the unlimited multiplication of needs.

The most effective means to neutralize energies is the principle of separation, which breaks the unity of desire and establishes human activity in a variety of sectors, to which a certain autonomy and a certain liberty become attached in isolation. Public sphere and private sphere: Marx retraced the historical genesis of this dissociation of two spheres between which there is a reciprocal negative determination.

Under cover of the illusory liberty of the private domain all the contradictions of the economic and the political constitute a burden on daily life and alter its lived sense. We dream of a domain reserved for leisure. In it can be read clearly the essence of repression: to index free aspirations to the very schema of servitude. Divided into work and leisure, daily life is organized from end to end in the same manner. Those who live parked in HLMs[2] or in the promiscuity of the production line can only dream, under the very sign of freedom, of overpopulated beaches and automobile horizons. The rupture between paradise and hell means that people can only dream of a paradise in the image of their hell.

The system of repression is rooted in the division of labour. But the violence which is exercised at the level of production and the human deficiency which results from piece-work are rarely lived as freedom: repression is therefore neither consumed nor consummated at this level (it does not here savour its own image, nor is it perfect at this level). More significant for us today is the repression exercised by the division of needs. For this plays on the illusion of the pleasure principle. All the prophets of the society of consumption boast of the liberation of needs and the promotion of an ever multiplied pleasure. It is as if modern man were endowed with virtual needs which only awaited products capable of satisfying them. To awaken these needs is to liberate mankind and tear it from centuries of repression. Liberate yourselves from your superego, enjoy life to the full. Of course, these neo-sorcerers are careful not to liberate mankind by means of an explosive end of happiness. The aim is to allow desires which were formerly blocked by mental obstacles (taboos, superego, guilt) to become crystallized onto objects or concrete instances in which the explosive force of desire is abolished and the repressive ritual function of social order materialized. Ever more free irrationality and the multiplication of needs at the base go hand in hand with more and more strict control at the summit.

Two aspects in solidarity with one another interest us here: the fact that the repression of desire occurs through the emancipation of needs (what Marcuse called repressive desublimation) – this emancipation is accompanied by a forced differentiation and ventilation of needs, their systematic alignment and dispersion across the array of products. In effect it is needs which are induced by products – or rather, since the latter are more coherent (needs are absolutely contingent), it is needs which flow back over them and insert themselves, broken up and separated from one another, in the array of objects (just as activities are necessarily inserted in the array of the division of labour – only escaping by inoffensive regression into *bricolage*). The system of individual needs is in a sense listed, classed and cut up by objects and products (including cultural products). It can therefore be controlled (which is the real aim of the system on the socio-economic level).

All this in order to clarify Marcuse's notion of repressive needs and to introduce a critique. Having seen that the most subtle modern alienation is tied to that level of interiorization of extra-economic violence described by repressive needs, Marcuse calls for the determinate negation of these needs and the raising up of new, conscious needs, concerted in their harmonious orientation towards an end; in other words, needs not complicit with the repressive reality principle, not complicit with an irrational pleasure principle, but, on the contrary, inaugurating a sort of rational and collective pleasure principle. But this is an illusion: on the one hand, if needs are historically determined (which Marcuse himself of course admits), it is difficult to see from whence these disalienated needs would arise. But above all, this Revolution of needs is ultimately no more than the modern version of the old idealist project of a moral education of humanity, a revolution of consciousnesses. We must be clear: neither needs nor any theory of needs will ever offer a perspective of disalienation or a revolutionary alternative because needs as such are immediately a product of repression, they are immediately broken up, divided, and systematically arrayed. To aim for the contrary of present repressive needs (their determinate negation) in their specificity is to risk inscribing oneself (negatively) in advance in a problematic which is already that of repression, to risk trapping oneself in a negativity without escape which at once forms part of the cultural mechanisms. In this sense, antitheatre is impossible despite Living Theatre or Grotowskian cleverness. It is the very institution of theatre which must be challenged, with its fundamental inscription of the scene as a place for the exercise of a separated activity, homologous to the separated institution of Power in every hierarchized society.

Similarly, it is not this or that need but the institution of need as separated end which must be denied. It is the same with need as with work: neither one nor the other exists. All that exists as social historical fact is the *division of labour* and the correlative *division of needs*. It is this double division which must be analyzed as the foundation of repression.

Every theory of needs, even those with revolutionary intentions, does no more than rearrange the contradiction between the social ends of order and the *anomie* of desire, or soften the code of controlled desublimation and provide a theoretical (ideological) basis for overrepression [*surrépression*].

By not locating repression in the rupture itself, in the segregation of individual and social practices, we are condemned to fight for the progressive liberalization of separated domains. For sexual freedom, for example, when this is tied to the exercise of sexuality as need, as separated activity, as performance, as perversion, as object of consumption, as individual regression (and not as desire). Similarly with the freedom to work. Similarly with holiday sunshine: is this bodily rehabilitation, beauty treatment, a condition of well-being? Yes, but these are *alibis*: they are separated ends, puritanical satisfactions, confined to holidays, parentheses around work, substitutes for desire. Holiday sunshine is repressive: its real function is the disavowal of the values of pleasure because it intervenes as the sign of an *absent* totality. Similarly with nudism: is this the truth of the body? Not at all. The truth of the body is desire, while nudism, by usurping the body as sign, disavows all the more, omits and censors nudity as flesh. Hypocrisy? No. Logic of repression.

Of course, repression is also exercised directly on certain contents (above all sexual). But what must be understood is that this is primarily a strategy which works through the systematic disjunction of the social body into zones, sectors, and dissociated activities, as occurs with the physical body, and through their assignment to a partial finality of *need*, in other words their devotion to satisfaction (or frustration) and not to pleasure and transgression. To take another example: I am alienated not as a consumer of free time or leisure, but to the extent that I experience as liberty a time formally opposed to labour time, to the extent that the very effect of liberty results from the process of dissociation of time into labour time/leisure time. The repression lies here and not in the eventual restriction of leisure time.

If we admit (with Marcuse) that, throughout the affluent society, repression is systematized by playing on needs, in other words on the principle of partial satisfaction tied to regression, and not at all on the principle of pleasure tied to transgression, then we admit also (against Marcuse) that all speculation on needs is pious and that only desire, in its irrational vehemence, in its heretical and insurrectional drive towards the totality, can offer a revolutionary alternative.

Having seen how the principle of repression is structurally organized, let us return quickly to its phantasmatic organization. The repressive efficacy of this society does not only derive from the paternal instance which founds the reality principle, institutes rational labour processes, bureaucratic processes of organization and political processes of power. Nor does it derive from the pure and simple substitution for this paternal instance of a gratifying maternal instance which is incarnate in the society of well-being and which enslaves energies in the name of a soft revolution. The efficacy of the system today derives from the fact that it plays on a *double instance*: there is still the traditional repressive Power, with its technical and social reality principle, class domination and the absolute finality of production, but this has learned not to impose itself brutally and learned to defray the risk of a brutal eruption of the repressed and the subversion of its order by allowing the *signs* of the pleasure principle to play at the very heart of repression. A whole litany of the gift, the offer, gratification, and fulfilment haunts publicity: see how the whole society adapts itself to you and your desires. You have not produced this object (you, salary worker), you have not bought it (you, salary worker), but you have expressed the desire and, through its engineers, technicians, and services, the global society (good Mother) has gratified you with it. It is clear that this litany is a *political* discourse, the tactic of which rests on a doubling of social reality into a real instance and an image, the former effacing itself behind the latter, becoming illegible and leaving only a schema of absorption in the maternal ambience.[3]

It is clear that, when publicity proposes in substance that society is totally adapted to you, so adapt yourself totally to it, the reciprocity is an illusion: an imaginary instance adapts itself to you, whereas in exchange you adapt yourself to an instance which is indeed real. Through the armchair which adapts to the shape of your body, YOU espouse the entire technical and political order of society. Society becomes maternal in order to better preserve an order of constraint. Moreover, behind this system of gratification, we see reinforced all the structures of authority: planning, centralization, bureaucracy – parties, apparatuses, States reinforce their hold behind this vast maternal image which renders less and less possible their (real) contestation.

Things may be formulated differently: the authoritarian repressive instance which exhausted itself attempting to reduce by force the contradictions between the reality principle and the pleasure principle, between individual drives and social ends, today manages to arrive at the same end by averting the drives in a system of happiness which is harmoniously integrated into the dynamics of production. The schemata of happiness, phantasms, and drives anterior to the reality principle are no longer sacrificed: they are aroused, provoked, and satisfied. *Repression operates by the detour of regression.* It thereby assists to reinvest in the reality principle all that which is anterior to and repressed by it, and which threatens to flow back over and submerge it.

A good example of this regression/repression is the eroticism in advertising (which haunts all of mass culture and which allows the good apostles of modernity to say that our society is on the way to eliminating sexual interdictions). Eroticism in advertising is never adult and genital. It is precisely, under the banner of genitality, the repression of all adult desire by (or through) the regressive schemata of pre-genital, maternal, nursing, and otherwise infantile homosexuality. The whole of repressed pre-genital sexuality comes back to haunt the signs of liberated genital sexuality. This is the real content of sexual liberation, and we see how repression is here much more profoundly accomplished than in puritanical repression. No more interdiction, censoring or moral ideology but instead the substitution of inoffensive infantile processes for any dangerous sexual irruption.

This repression by infantilization involves a powerful reactivation of play (irony or anti-advertising which has no critical value whatsoever but a *paracritical* value integrated in advance into the advertising effect, along with the obligatory smile). In the society of consumption, everything becomes a sign to be played with and consumed, including the most radical critique of this society. Nor does repression escape. While fighting on the barricades, the students enlivened themselves with their acoustic image being played on transistors. Everywhere this society regards itself, but the humour with which it sees itself is not at all critical: it is the humour of *LUI* magazine, Godard films; a complacent lucidity which is the number one value of spontaneous intellectual discourse.

Better still (and it is at this point that the system subtly closes in on itself and becomes almost inescapable), this play of distancing is the specific mode of con- sumption of the *culpability* which is attached to the infantile regression which is implied by consumption itself. Traditional, open repression was carried out in the name of a puritan morality. Modern repression is carried out in the name of play. It operates in play (combinatory liberty) as it flourishes in the mass-media, in erotic play, etc., and as it culminates in the critical play of the intelligentsia; it operates in the play to which desire definitively resigns itself. But this play is far from being the reconciliation of desire and the reality principle, as it is in the case of children or in works of art. On the contrary, it masks the intense culpability which is attached to this type of regressive gratification behind the mere signs of detachment. Thereby averted in the signs of play, culpability is consumed like any other object.

It is perhaps even the end of the end of consumption for a particular social group, namely intellectuals. Culpability is the order of the day; its psychological exegesis is undertaken everywhere. It will also be necessary to undertake its socio- logy. In other words, to analyse among other things how it is that culpability can come to sustain the very existence of a group and come to be exploited by it for cultural ends.[4] For the intelligentsia in particular culpability is a distinctive value. Of course it has individual psychological foundations, but it is above all *socially orchestrated* like any other cultural trait of behaviour or clothing, in the end like an effect of fashion – in other words, like an element of the social code.

There is a culpability-value in the Western intellectual milieu in the same way that there is a goat-value in Kikuyu society. This is a properly social *exchange value* which has nothing to do with the neurotic dispositions of individuals. This culpability does not fall within the province of psychoanalysis: it is an element of the group economy. It falls within the province of social crisis or of cultural con- tact with other groups. One thinks of the delicious discontent that is sought in Living Theatre or in the political masochism of Left intellectuals, etc. More gene- rally, shame is a number one journalistic value. It is a collective drug (which never engages responsibility): hence the great campaigns over the Wall of Shame, Biafra: the shame of civilized men, etc. Everyday consumption and advertising are themselves impregnated with shame; this is one of the aspects of the discon- tent of civilization. The collision of two moral imperatives, the ascetic ethos and the modern imperative of pleasure, finds its resolution in a compromise: enjoyment indexed to blame – shameful enjoyment – the reintegration of the failure to reach orgasm into the enjoyment, etc. Consumption is *also* this. Advertising includes a whole lexicon of denied pleasure.

It is therefore not only the conjuncture of an isolated group that we are describ- ing; it is the contradiction of a whole civilization that is expressed, as always, by the marginal class of intellectuals. But at the same time this class grasps hold of this contradiction as a distinctive value, monopolizing it, manipulating it, and thereby assuring a part of its own power.

All this defines, in contrast to the radical negativity of desire, a secondary negativity of play which today becomes autonomous everywhere but especially as a *paracritical subculture* among intellectuals. In this manner the transgression of hierarchical social values turns into the game of a cultural elite, the subversive appeal to happiness turns into the game of social differentiation. This is the proper coronation of repression, in which the repressive instance and the forces of transgression coexist in a truly conjugal neurosis.

Where to from here? Is there a point external to the system when the latter can congratulate itself for both playing and suborning in its very functioning the forces which threaten disruption? What kind of political action is possible? Revolution? The principle of Revolution, as it is founded on a historical dialectic of resolution of social contradictions, is a *rational* principle. It is situated entirely in the field of the reality principle. It has direct purchase on the traditional repressive type of society because it belongs to the same theoretical and political field, but does it still have purchase on a new type of repressive society in which the fundamental contradictions remain but masked and suborned by regressive processes of play, and in which repressive adjustment gives way to consented adjustment, to a systematic complicity and to that ambient euphoria which we discussed above?

A completely new situation is created, a situation of *perfect repression* which, by virtue of the fact that it operates beyond politics, calls for a transpolitical type of intervention. This is the type of intervention that we saw emerge in the month of May, where in the end objective contradictions and their dialectical overcoming were hardly spoken of but where we saw the eruption of a principle anterior (or ulterior) to the reality principle, intervening all at once in the form of living contestation of the system, and thereby denouncing it, upsetting it, and aiming more to subvert it and block it than to explode its contradictions in order to dialectically resolve them. Before the principles of repressive Power and Revolution, conjugated in their antagonism, a third principle arose: the principle of Subversion.

In other words, once more: hitherto the revolutionary dynamic was able to hold itself up before an established, conservative order as the principle of change, movement and social progress (at once symbolic and economic: liberation of the productive forces). But Revolution can no longer be inscribed as the principle of change before a society which has embraced every ideology of change and growth, whose repressive modality (the modernist reality principle) is that of functioning, of productivity, of innovation, whose mode of apparition is that of a perpetual flux of signs (fashion in all its aspects, consumption/consummation in the broadest sense); on the contrary, Revolution will take the form of interruption, rupture, dysfunction, and blockage. When a system manages to maintain its equilibrium by its own continual breakdown, when it manages to digest its own contradictions and profits from its own crises, when the hierarchy of functions and relations takes the form of objective reason, and when sexual liberty itself is a byproduct of productivity, what remains but to interrupt it and raise the almost blind demand of the real pleasure principle, the radical demand of transgression, against the massive collusion under the sign of satisfaction? This is what appeared as the style of intervention of the active elements in May.

The historical possibilities must be thought according to the forms which put the accent on rupture rather than on continuity with past history, on negation rather than on the positive, on difference rather than progress.

In a society which is no longer exactly a society of repression but a society of persuasion and of the dissuasion of individual ends, only subversion of an instinctual order can constitute a point external to the system. This subversion is nevertheless also political by virtue of the fact that it intervenes in a political field. But its register is not that of conscious finality nor that of contradiction, its mode is not dialectical. Its negativity is radical. It aims not at the overcoming of its contradictions but at the abolition of separations. It aims to restore the totality, not by a dialectical labour on the separated elements but by a pure act of critical regression.

For it must be said that (as we saw in May) the contestation of this repressive/regressive society is undertaken with the aid of schemata largely borrowed from values and models anterior to the reality principle: the refusal of work, of organization, the drive to happiness, enjoyment without restraint, etc.[5] This may explain the transfer of this radical subversive action to a not exactly political class, namely the young; in other words to a class with only latent economic and social responsibility, a class which does not yet confront the economic system in its real contradictions but only as a system of values and of (counter-)finalities. The concept of transgression, moreover, refers expressly to archaic societies anterior to the contradictions of our economic order. The highly integrated primitive hierarchical order is a stranger to revolution but does presuppose transgression which is ritual and periodic, a kind of social menstruation which is cyclical like the order which it periodically inverts. In our rationalized society as well, transgression is largely integrated into rites of rebellion (those of the critical intelligentsia – see above) or of revolution (rigorous socialism). But this society remains inferior to primitive societies in its real power of integration: it by and large controls conscious oppositional processes but not yet unconscious oppositional processes. Transgression runs through these like a savage resurgence, like an irreducible which is no longer that of the moral and political conscience confronting the powers that be, but that of the vital impulse confronting the vital repression, not of this or that political system but of the social order as order, and not of the order in its contradictions but in its very coherent finality. We will see more and more of these unpredictable transgressions and these convulsions in the system of values.

The political problem is to analyse how this radical negativity can be articulated with the objective contradictions, not from a metaphysical or metapsychological point of view, but in the reality of the social classes which support them and the social struggles which they undertake.

Theoretical analysis must no longer take its point of departure from the hypothesis of a polar antagonism between class society and Revolution, but from the three terms: class Institution/Revolution/Subversion, and from the complex relations between the three.

Translated by Paul Patton

Notes

Originally published as 'Le Ludique et le Policier', *Utopie* 2/3 (mai 1969): 3–15.

1. *Trans. note*. Compagnie républicaine de sécurité (state security police force).
2. *Trans. note*. Habitation à loyer modéré (public housing).
3. In his recent book *La Révolte Contre le Père* (Paris: Payot, 1968), Gérard Mendel reaches a similar conclusion that social Power in industrial society represents a combination of both parents in the collective conscience.
4. It is in this double sense that we understand *consommation*: culpability at once savoured as an object of satisfaction and delectation and, this shared pleasure merges into collective value in complicity with the group and cultural privilege.
5. It is perhaps a law that there is, in the same domain of civilization, and thus in the same symbolic field, an affinity and collusion between order and disorder, between Law and subversion. To a society with a regressive tendency perhaps corresponds a degeneration of the regressive type, that is, a pure transgression, and no longer a historical 'revolution' and political consciousness.

Mass (Sociology of)

Mass Languages

The languages of propaganda and advertising are mass languages, constituting the medium of a widespread socialization of messages which appear simultaneously with the advent, at the turn of the nineteenth century, of a practice of mass politics (through the course of the French Revolution and universal suffrage) and of mass production (through the course of the Industrial Revolution). Yet neither one nor the other – propaganda nor advertising – comes, respectively, fully into its own until after the October Revolution and the global crisis of 1929. And, at the same time, their respective fields (and their language) are brought so close that they merge. It is clear that advertising arises as a factor of the rescuscitation and consolidation of neo-capitalism, and is thus directly like a political practice. As for propaganda, it can be defined from the beginning as a true *marketing* and *merchandising* of the key ideas of men of politics and parties, with their 'brand images'.

More and more, propaganda and advertising converge today in a global strategy of human relations, in a style of communications and language. And it is in this contemporary convergence that they define a type of society such as our own in which there is no longer a difference between the economic and the political, because the same language dominates throughout them; a society, then, where 'political economy', literally speaking, is at last fully realized. There have always been techniques of commercial distribution or of political persuasion, but advertising and propaganda do not truly appear until a period when language aims at a total public and becomes by the same token totalitarian. This is the era of the media.

A Structure of Modernity

In a first phase, having been based upon a psychology of conditioned reflex, of anxiety and electroshock, that is to say, upon a mechanistic and metallurgical technique of human relations, this mass language is today oriented towards a psychology of contact, dialogue and feedback; in other words it is based upon a cybernetic technique of information understood as a system of integral relations. But, in any case, it is defined by a decisive rupture between a category of senders and a mass of receivers (citizens or consumers), a rupture which is distinct from the circuit of the right to speak amongst the members of a traditional group. With this type of mediatic language thus appears a characteristic structure of modernity: the technical and social division of communication and messages, which go to sanction and intensify the technical and social division involved in the production of material goods. With advertising and propaganda, linked to the emergence of the media and of the modern forms (press, cinema, radio, television), a collective regulation of unidirectional signs is erected with no possibility of any real response possible. (Who responds to the messages of advertising and propaganda?) It is in this sense that their language is 'totalitarian'. This unilateral regulation joins together with that of the production and distribution of material goods: a real political economy of the sign.

An Operational Language

In the functional order, what characterizes this type of language is the predominance of what Jakobson calls the 'conative function': the targeting of the receiver. These are 'operational' languages that aim to redirect the behaviour of the receiver. Of course, they also have a referential function: the one refers to consumer goods, the other to the management of the public entity. They pretend to instruct, explain, to speak the truth – they will always retreat, but seldom decisively and in one stroke, behind this value of information and objectivity. But the objective reference of this discourse, of which it speaks, largely disappears behind the mode in which it speaks: the imperative mode, the seductive mode. It is necessary to win support, to force consensus and, maximally – which is increasingly apparent with the current intensification of the media – the content is no more than an excuse for this function of seduction. The German term that designates the ensemble of these practices says it quite well: *werben* originally signified erotic and amorous solicitation. Commercial or political manipulation aiming to traffic in the dissemination of such a product or ideology is, without doubt, the manifest discourse of advertising and propaganda. On this level, then, their efficacy is completely relative: propaganda convinces bit by bit, its contents nullify, in a sense, one another. Advertising, we begin to see, does not sell (this is the least of its failings), but this does not matter: its strategy lies elsewhere. It is the generalized social integration of the *mise en scène* of all human relations according to the code they impose, of social control generalized through the injunctive or seductive mode, of abstraction and of spectacle (behind the ideology of contact, dialogue and solicitude). It is this form, that is to say, not at all such and such content, but a definite – totalitarian – form of social relations, that such language imposes.

Beyond Truth and Falsehood

At this point, advertising and propaganda mark a decisive (possibly definitive) phase in the history of communication. Western rationality has always been based, as regards discourse, upon the criteria of truth and falsehood. Now, this neo-language, which has become the socially dominant language (it occupies not only the traditional fields of commerce or politics, but all the spheres of culture and social communication), is beyond or before truth and falsehood. It totally changes the traditional foundations of truth and falsehood, as it does not thrive on objective reality; rather, it thrives on codes and models. It does not thrive on reference or veracity; instead, it thrives on actual seduction, desire, ephemerality and, in the end, the code.

It is not at all that we are 'fooled': the objection that propaganda and advertising consist of lying, bluffing, and mystification is the weakest and most naïve that we could raise. And so much so the complementary question, the veritable sea monster of the human sciences: do people believe it or not? Do advertisers and propagandists believe what they say? (They will be half-forgiven.) Do consumers and voters not believe what they are told? (They will be half-saved.) But the question does not lie there. One might be able to say, like D.J. Boorstin in *The Image*, that the genius of Barnum, or of Hitler, was to discover not how easy it is to mislead the public, but how much the public loves to be fooled. Or further, that the most serious problems posed by advertising derive less from the unscrupulousness of those who fool us than from our pleasure in being fooled; they proceed less from the desire to seduce than from the desire to be seduced. Seductive hypothesis, but one that does not go deep enough: there is no manipulation of truth and falsehood at this level of language as it effaces, or radically displaces, the very conditions of truth or falsehood.

Advertising, for example, makes objects into events, but it constructs them as such on the basis of the elimination of their objective characteristics. It constructs them as spectacular current events, as myth, as model. The media do the same with 'historic' events: they construct them as models. They eventually construct them in all instances as models of simulation; propaganda does the same with ideas and concepts of social and political practice. 'Modern advertising comes into its own when an ad no longer functions as a spontaneous announcement, but becomes a new *fabrication*' (Boorstin). These models are not false: they have their logic and their coherence, but no longer derive them from ordinary reality – they come from their own code, becoming the reality principle. The deep seduction of these languages doubtless comes from this hypercoherence of a code, of a mythical and structural treatment where seduction can at last freely exercise itself, where desire can finally be fulfilled without the constraints of reality. (Simulation is also the foundation of all cybernetic and operational research, and one knows what social power of control this constitutes today.) Advertisers and propagandists are thus mythic operators, but not liars. This is more serious in a way because if they were merely liars, it would be easy to unmask them. Thus, all their art consists in the invention of persuasive displays that are neither true nor false.

In this way, their language refers entirely to a historical and social mutation which is accomplished under the logic of the sign. Mass communication is beyond truth and falsehood in the way that fashion is beyond beauty and ugliness, as political 'reason' is beyond good and evil, and as objects are beyond utility and uselessness. All the great humanistic criteria of value, all those of a civilization of moral, aesthetic, practical judgement, fade away in our system of images and signs.

If this language of operational seduction is a mythic discourse, one could ask where the principle of its real efficacy lies. It is that of prophetic speech, of the *self-fulfilling prophecy*: 'the advertiser is master of a new art: the art of rendering things true in asserting that they are. It is an adept in the technique of prophecy who can accomplish this'. If, then, this language has its 'veracity', it is of a completely different type of verification that it concerns. Advertising does not suppose a prior reality, not even an object, but rather an ulterior confirmation, by virtue of the reality of a sign that it emits. It makes the object into a pseudo-event that will become the real event of daily life through the belief of the consumer in its discourse. The verification of its discourse is that part of consensus that it provokes, and its day of reckoning is the same as its unriddling: perfect definition of the magical sign, omnipotence of the artefact of the sign over the end of the world. Thus, the polls are where the most modern face of propaganda is legible: impossible to know if they reflect a public opinion or if the real vote is only the latest poll – but it is no longer a real event, it is nothing but the image of the model of anticipated simulation.

The Internal Logic of this Neo-language

To this displacement of truth and falsehood and inversion of the referential and the code corresponds a completely different apparatus of the discourse from that of traditional logic.

Tautology

Logical articulation is replaced by tautology: 'Omo, there, that's washing'; 'The majority, that's you,' etc. This general schema culminates in the pure and simple incantation of the brand name or political slogan. All signs amount to one sign that equals itself: the brand or the slogan. It's on this recognizable sign, incessantly reduplicating itself, that this discourse comes to be indexed, contrary to open logical discourse. And it is this secret tautology, even if it wraps itself in significations and very rich rhetorical figures, that produces its efficacious causality and verisimilitude. It is this internal repetition that induces the 'magical' repetition of discourse in the event.

Paralogia of Detail

Advertising is a total discourse of details, marginal differences, and partial truths reified in totality. It's the litany of the cigar lighter, the rhetoric of the accessory.' In propaganda as well, technique consists in the orchestration of such detail, such selective aspects of reality, to the saturation of the ideological field. (Racist propaganda is exaltation derived from one, and only one, differential characteristic – race or blood – in order to make a total ideology.) There also, the logic of the whole and the part substitutes for that of truth and falsehood. The logic of displacement and substitution takes the place of dialectical articulation.

Paradox of the Conjunction of Incompatibles and the Identity of Contradictions

'At 140 km/h, you go faster in a Renault 16'. 'Three razors in one: when Phillips outdoes Phillips'. 'Living in the year 2000, today'. 'Invisibly dressed'.

This principle of magical synthesis, itself the corollary of tautology, is revealed in politics as the very language of terrorism and deterrence: it is the famous *Peace is war, war is peace*[1] of George Orwell's *Nineteen Eighty-Four* or, further, 'clean bomb', 'harmless fallout', and, once again, 'the majority, that's you'. Hypnotic language that no longer knows contradiction or negativity and thus returns to what Freud described as primary process: 'Thoughts which are mutually contradictory make no attempt to do away with each other, but persist side by side. They often combine to form condensations, *just as though there were no contradiction between them*, or arrive at compromises such as our conscious thoughts would never tolerate but such as are often admitted in our actions'.[2]

One sees this paradox again in the magical return of 'anti-advertising', which does nothing but mimic the critical distance *vis-à-vis* itself the better to pursue its objective – a bit like the artifice of the censor saying that 'one dreams within the dream'. It is by this same principle of total compatibility on the basis of the pure and simple manipulation of signs that the discourse can short-circuit and annex every other kind of discourse: scientific (biology of enzymes, technology, history), poetic and cultural, revolutionary discourse, discourse of the unconscious, objective discourse, critical discourse – all can be reintegrated as simulacra and serve as an alibi function for the mythic discourse.

Abolition of Syntax

This is possibly the most characteristic tendency. 'Persil washes whiter' is not a sentence that is properly spoken, an articulate utterance. It is a frozen syntagm, identification, a solitary, full sign, a sentenceless indicative that declares itself an imperative. The same thing for 'change in continuity' or 'great party of the workers'. On the level of these language blocs, all discursivity is lost. Full signs, closed, indissociable, replaceable one by another within the indefinite paradigm that abolishes all syntax, whose actual function is to abolish syntax as a shifting dimension where meaning is made and unmade. Moreover, there is a proliferation in the neo-language of prefixes, suffixes, superlatives (anti-, neo-, super-, etc.), generators of reflexive significations, of a desymbolized punchcard language.

The Monopoly of Speech

All these modalities place this discourse beyond reach of the game of logical reason, dialectic of sense and contradiction. It is in this way that it is terroristic, for it is here, through this manipulation of language on the level of the code, that it forbids all reciprocity of communication and any response to its messages (other than those already coded with its own signs). Certainly, advertising and propaganda *also* transmit ideological contents: dominant moral values, political dogmas – but once again, this 'manifest' ideology collides with individual or very complex collective systems of defence that are more solid than one thinks. It is true that everyone 'believes it', and that no one basically disbelieves. On the other hand, that's where this language is particularly efficacious; that's where everyone is vulnerable because it is a matter of the very structure of exchange: in its form, in this destructuration of traditional logic, in the imposition of this fixity of a social relation (always the same ones speak) and of this opaque circularity of signs (always the same signs sign). Nebulousness of closed signs, which can only be unilaterally deciphered, which are not any longer exchangeable between persons as in genuine symbolic discourse, and which really do not exchange either the role of sender or receiver. One sees that the neo-language, behind its ideology of dialogue and mass communication, prolongs and sanctions the dominant social abstraction, and contributes to the broader reproduction of a society of monopolized speech and meaning, reinforcing by its very articulation the power of the ones and the irresponsibility of the others.

Translated by Ben Freedman

Notes

Originally published as 'Masse (Sociologie de)', *in Encyclopedia Universalis France*, Vol. 17 (1975), pp. 394–7. Reprinted *in Encyclopedia Universalis France*, Vol. 14 (1990), pp. 680–3.

1. *Trans. note.* English in the original.
2. *Trans. note.* Sigmund Freud, *The Interpretation of Dreams*, James Strachey (trans.), P.F.L. Vol. 4, Harmondsworth: Penguin, 1986, p. 755.

PART III

THE POETRY OF THEORY

Stucco Angel

Translator's Preface

In the case of Baudrillard's sequence of poems 'Stucco Angel', the difficulties inherent in translating poetry deserve special mention: not because they are insuperable (they are), but because they lead directly to what seems, arguably, to be the poems' point. For the reader puzzling over the meaning of Baudrillard's lines, language is not the primary issue, and I have stayed close to the French for reasons that play on the specificity of Baudrillard's choices; even so, much of the play on sound is irrecoverable and this is a loss, particularly if one accepts Mike Gane's (1991: 118–25) argument about the anagrammatic significance of the poems' sound patterns in the original French. What can be conveyed, however, is the poems' insistence on an ambiguous literality, their play on the specificity of the word, and the illusionary nature of the referent. This play is inherent in the suggestion, present in the collection's title and implicit elsewhere, that the poems as a sequence respond at least in part to a representation of reality that is in some sense before the poet, who perceives a world whose naturalness is regulated by a set of constructed images.

Although, or perhaps because, the poems are at once precise and impressionistic, there is throughout a fluid, if apparently arbitrary, movement between fixed points. Certain elements recur across the sequence, indeed the elements themselves (water, fire, etc.) flow around such elements, which include cardinal points, body parts (and associated disorders, conveyed in precise medical or anatomical terminology), and specific natural phenomena: birds and trees of various (and invariably named) kinds, both apparently points of contact between the earth and the changing sky. At the same time, constructed and containing forms are present, though they are empty: the 'quadrature' of walls, bedframes, chairs. In the context of such incipient verticality, shared by the trees as well, the flight of birds suggests a mediating force between distant or fixed points, but the poems routinely posit such spatial mediation only to leave its grounds, so to speak, up in the air.

The poems present a kind of 'superficial abyss', and can be illuminated by a companion text, Baudrillard's remarks on Renaissance *trompe-l'oeil* in *Seduction* as 'enchanted simulation' where, as Gane points out, some lines of these poems are scattered. In the representational space of *trompe-l'oeil*, objects are context-less, everything is reduced to the status of artefact in an illusionary, simulated space. 'Stucco Angel' may be read as both a meditation on, and an enactment of, a *trompe-l'oeil* world in which objects become 'blank, empty signs that bespeak a social, religious or artistic anti-ceremony or anti-representation', and it is for this reason that they must be 'juxtaposed at random'. As Baudrillard pursues the implications of this in *Seduction*, it becomes clear that such objects are no longer objects: 'they describe a void, an absence, the absence of every representational hierarchy that organizes the elements of a tableau, or for that matter, the political order' (Baudrillard 1990: 60). The activity of translating such a weightless world, suspended as it is against a vertical backdrop, is both exposed and exposing: to the extent that translation re-represents the text, it tends to exert its own gravita-tional pull – and here, against an 'object' whose mode is precisely to resist. Translation, thus, by being effectively prevented from leading away, leads us to the representational issues central to the poems.

Sophie Thomas

References

Baudrillard, Jean (1990) *Seduction*, trans. Brian Singer, Montréal: New World Perspectives.

Gane, Mike (1991) *Baudrillard's Bestiary: Baudrillard and Culture*, London and New York: Routledge.

Stucco Angel

And they saw a stucco angel whose extremities were joined along one curve.

Baroque Apocalypse, sixteenth century

(1)

If off-stage falls
speaking
this upright one
among dissimilar friends and who
have been chosen the sleeping
buzzard that was flying
concentrically
in view of an order
at the Sun's pinnacle
at the mercy of the Sun
on the look-out, without eyes,
without consciousness,
on this Persian stake
the Taillades – or
if intractability
must be renounced,
it is that retracted, disunited, and
unable to separate from one another –
the one arrives on time
in a trance, the other
having maintained a singular limit –
the balance is no longer in us
as it would be for he who wants it,
but that thirst has again
questioned patience.
But what we no longer want
will change no more
leaving us alone
while haunting us.

(2)

From very high
the white-tailed eagle

destroys itself and
returns to what it was.
But the hunger of others
has changed everything.
In the fields of dung
winter has preceded us.
Under inarticulate streets
the real fire, or
the revolt,
from North to South.
To a water source
bitter from cold
in the grass
everything is fixation
abscess of signs
and of broken lines
but out of sight and
bitter from heat
or preceding us
or having rejoined
what haunts
and represents us.

(3)

Distant
is memory
but the sun is near
the mask nearer still
and soft
the recollection of gestures
but stronger
joy
that differs
in crazy determination
underground
or from West to East
like blood
the white of forces
naked and divining
of evil
by this heat –
or from clouds
disjointed
reappears
a second femininity –

nakedness is
fluid like
a definitive childhood
where double thoughts
take root
in uterine coolness
and tenacious femininity.

(4)

The water is so clear
that animals
can draw it forth.
All is exact
or brought to life
on stage
not far from human understanding
or under the scythe
under the ashes
under the residues.
Striated muscles
innervate the overturned
ground. The water itself
is innervated
by the terms of evil.
And nothing is separated.
All is exact like
blood under the nails.
And so alternate
imagined things
that contain their
own emptiness, where shines
immersed like
a chair
the gestural sword of
the Sun.

(5)

If the very paths
soluble even before
the absence of wind
on the water where
they hunt, and where
the animals they hunt
resemble them

the amorous spider
immobile
in the direction of the wind
so fructifying
like an iced cider
in the sensual space
of a cellar – for
coolness is a
passion and your hands are
alive and slender like
birds of passage –
or multiplied
by the falling night and
steamed by the ground, or
exonerated by the sun, and
cast in nonchalance
to the ground – but
to another verticality
than that
of walls – to the image
of others, not of the self, and
in unreality of others
if need be, but outside of
ourselves, always, toward
the reconciliation of
centrifugal forces taken
in the absurdity of landscape
what then?
We laugh through the oral
rent on the threshold of
de-motion, for the Medusas
of the notion are
the will paralysed by
the ruse of broken lines.

(6)

The underside of the sky
engraved on copper
and clouding over the water even
between the end of the halls
and the flower market
when one overcomes the image
the ones from others
the eyes open – but
without breaking the symmetry

and yet
the sparkle of the eye comes
from the game of opposite thoughts and
from the uncertainty of the will, and
if in the morning our
dreams will be explained – why
walk all night?
Up to the frailest meninx
of trees, of steps,
from near or far
it is the faithfulness of one only
or for simulants, the winter,
the shame made
of the softness of
a foreign body.
Genital scorsenaires,
perfumed
by desire
the synclinal bird calls
its eagle-song
anticlinal from the
forest.

(7)

Behind the shutters
without shutters
loving feverishness
second limitation –
and everything is reversible.
They are stucco figures
specious and strident –
alleyways open
onto transverse courtyards
to receive us.
It is the exact number
of steps that diminish
just close to here
but high in the sky
the rain falls
in one direction or the other
as I turn the palm
of the hand toward
the outside – as one does
to those who sleep
with eyes open.

(8)

On stage or
under walls violently lit
but retained
but preserved, and
never touching the ground
animal peripeteia – suppleness
mental peripeteia – the dance
and the battles
neither victory nor defeat,
that's what war is,
and the spirals of tiling
are these
in any event – but
fleeing beneath them like
an alternative dream
cursive or discursive
the lines of flight
flat surfaces
raw flesh, balancing
between twin lanterns.
And the light is so cold
that it differentiates wine
from water
in the same glass.
They are the swallows who
return to whence they came.
And the fire goes out quietly
like a fire that
goes out quietly.

(9)

The voice also
changes clime.
Birds forestall those
who see them, the fastest ones.
It is an innovation of our sleep.
Absent one is like
the voice in aphonia
or the uninhabited house
amid deaf music
and bursts of glass –
bare walls without faith nor
anything but earthenware tiles

instead of being of flesh –
uninhabited, but
the grass is soft
to the workings of thighs, and more
than time and space
separates us
the anomaly of mechanical jewels
as far as an iron bedstead
out in the country
disused
or high in the sky – as
you wish, the icy wind
clearly this time
the walls are standing
their shadow prolongs
those who think of them.

(10)

A clock without hands
imposes time but
leaves the hour to be divined.
Darkness is simple or
the contradictory one
of green curtains.
Water is soft to the touch
like a natural death.
Outside, warm
is the sapwood of ash trees and
the belly of cocks
friable under the fingers
and translucent
under the eyelids of the mask
like the outerwings of dead
butterflies – warmer than
the interior stratifications of irises
the vitreous humour
of eyes –
hot and asexual
the night
like an eye
without eyelashes
like a window
without ivy,
naked and asexual
the surface of the ground

that escapes
the quadrature of walls

(11)

Not only in their eyes
the smoke dispelled
the prairial smoke
and all the water lives
derisively
the face of yours
but in those of animals
from one bank to the other
and in each curve or
median of your body
all is clear
the deep grasses burn
the light changes
each cloud has its personal repose
that of March
a dry imagination
hour by hour
the time to see each other
and the multiplicity is in the nerves
that of objects preceded
in our own eyes
by their negative reflection
or the partial light
of a prison-house
unreadable harm
involuted from the left
from the right
each summer
each winter.

(12)

Bitter
on gloved hands
the artificial light
thc North
but a single cry, childhood
is like a bare throat
the Orient
thirst and
the satisfaction of thirst

the full heat
the aberration of strength
the height of the summer –
even empty the scene retains
the possibility of leaving it –
meanwhile inside is
that fallible
without thinking of it, and the soft
wind, tangential to the walls,
to itself – elasticity
as through a smoked glass
of the uneven voice
of the odd step
the Occident
play cry
our nails are so long
that the four corners of the sky
hang on like torn up
earth – and
neither ground nor sky, but wanted
the sun outside
not only gestures are
calculated, even the hands
are jealous
of each other.

(13)

Named
fire by euphony
or differently
that which walks and flies
hewn rock
the awning for shade
the cry of the blackbird
the white of teeth
coolness
this is like nakedness
under the dry earth
or rivalry
playing played disfigured
according to the brown veil
behind the poplars
or the felinity
of lightened rocks
of fluid hedges

of walls of heat
outside
neither the wind stops at the corners
nor the blood goes far
all forces diverge
adversity makes me
think
sleep
when everything is so beautiful –
and generosity also
against derision – but
another says it
it is the Sun that leads
it is the calm of the spirit.

(14)

Toward the cold abscess
of insomnia to the
compass card
hard and analytical
that attracts the dead – steel
in spongy earth
or
to the open sky
heard to neigh
the habitual horseman of March
without laughing
on flying bridges
and the switches in
neutral – everyday is
like an agitated leaf
in the small hours of day –
but is it that one loves, or
the equality of race?
The tree itself is enucleated
by the absence of water, and
the thinness of leaves and
of nerves – yet there are
neither leaves nor nerves –
only dryness passes
through us – and there is
neither face nor profile –
it falls short of all
our bodies.

(15)

Clairperdue
on each phalanx
of the child without hands
in the quick lime
iron hooks
and the afternoon fire
of winter in the unsociable
eyes of dogs
the substance of what they are
and that a madman hasn't the right
to change – that one
hunger in the belly and
their image facing
it is the asymmetrical ash
open to the axe
sex of rocks
of chairs of walls
even of night
or isolated resting
violet are the fire-dogs
the straw matting crunches
and opens the windows
on the uprooted trees
the mute fingers too
of mutes pretend
to read.

(16)

Ex-inscribed on the window
the taste of steel
the sheets are warm
they frighten the dogs
the image itself is withdrawn
it is the water that is
retained by the trees
the day goes – and a door
turns upon itself – but
if the table forgets to be
square, how to turn
around?
Dog stopped short
again by inertia and
the haste of the Sun is

inhabitual – but we
are immobile, walking
toward the wall facing
affluent neighbourhoods
the end of the war, looking
on faces for what
the Greeks read
in the entrails of pigs,
because of whatever end
one has already dreamed –
the imagination amassing
ingenuously
the illusion of courage.

(17)

A bird, is she or
deer dress
or clover smoke
or doll of medlar fruit
or like a wild cat
imaginary with a piercing cry
in the perfect darkness
the föhn or the violent wind
less far and brief
but far as if it were yesterday
clearer
from the animality of a new book
the unmown grass
any day
by the clouds of pink stucco
and soft psychological penetration
white mass
without audience
then the red and green dawn
that doesn't conduct noise
separates us
you run right ahead
secret sign of solicitude
and so everywhere one wants to be
present before having
arrived when it is others
who speak but
one has not yet finished with
real hair
real hands

the very evidence
A bird, is she or
deer dress
or clover smoke
or doll of medlar fruit
it is her
unlyrical and surreptitious
less far and brief, but far
as if it were yesterday
it is her of whom
I would never have had the idea
on my own.

Translated by Sophie Thomas

Note

Originally published as *L'Ange de Stuc*, Paris: Éditions Galilée, 1978.

PART IV

POLITICAL BANKRUPTCY ON THE LEFT AND RIGHT

The Divine Left

1. The Cavalry of the Union of the Left

a. March 1977. The Enchanted Battle or the Final Flute

A spectre haunts the spheres of power: communism. But a spectre haunts the communists themselves: power.

Everything is faked in the contemporary political scene, ruled by a simulacra of revolutionary tension and power grabs by the communists (and the Left in general); in fact, behind every *mise en scène* to which the communists continue to devote themselves in order to form a front against the Right and thereby preserve the entire edifice, a negative obsession with power drives and gives them a constantly renewed inertial force. It is the shame of the revolution that stimulates them. They are not alone in this because the political has escaped everyone, and even the Right has no resort. However, in the Leninist perspective to which everyone adheres (and to which they themselves believe faithfully), the communists can be found to have historically always appeared as politicos, as professionals in the business of taking power. It is thus with them that political failure and decay are most flagrant. Afraid of the power that cripples even the perspective opened up by Sanguinetti in the *True Report on the Last Chance to Save Capitalism in Italy*, the communists relieve the dominant class of the exercise of power and the political management of capital (the last Italian elections [1976] unmasked the utopia still nourished by the old cynical idealism of the class struggle).

What is the source of this impotence, this castration? Who knotted their needle? What kind of enchantment leads them to always fail so close to their goal, not as a challenge, like the long-distance runner who in his solitude chooses to lose and thus reject the rules of the game – no, why do they irresistibly fail to take power? Why do they desperately put on the brakes, cartoon-like, when they see the abyss of power?

Italian Communist Party secretary Enrico Berlinguer declares: 'We don't have to be afraid of the communists taking power in Italy'. An ideally ambiguous formula because it signifies:

- there is nothing to fear because the communists, if they come to power, won't change the fundamental capitalist mechanism in the least;
- there is no risk that they will ever come to power because they don't want to;
- but also: in fact power, a real power, no longer exists – there is no power anymore – and therefore no risk that someone will take or retake it;
- and again: I (me, Berlinguer) am not afraid to see the communists take power in Italy – which appears logical, or rather evident, but at bottom not really because that could mean the contrary (no need for psychoanalysis to see that): I AM AFRAID to see the communists take power in Italy (and there are good reasons for that, albeit for a communist).

All of this is simultaneously true. It is the secret of a discourse whose ambiguity translates itself into the drift of power. The impossibility of a determined discursive position. The impossibility of a determined position of power. Zero degree of political will. The parties all bear the costs of this liquidation, but the communists are the ones who most cruelly testify to this abolition of the will to political power.

The affair of the 'false' pamphlet from Moscow to the Portuguese Communist Party on the most effective means of taking power. The incredible *naïveté* of all the actors in this vaudeville. It had to be the thwarted Left who launched this hoax in order to resuscitate a political energy long since lost by the communists. For a long time, in the shadows of flowering communist parties, there has only been a virgin Left who waits to be violated by the Right. Was this a real document or a fake? It doesn't matter, because evidently the converse is true: we know that the communists were long since programmed to not take power. It was the best example of an offensive simulation in the form of a false inversion: 'Moscow directives to global communist parties on the most effective means to never take power'.

Against all faking in the political sphere, which revolves around the idea of the subversion of the existing order by the Communist Party, against the temptation to see everyone as complicit, this destructive simulation had to be introduced – a falsehood that takes the entire model of contemporary political simulation in reverse.

They themselves (because everything happens as if they knew what they were doing) put forth all kinds of good reasons why – in terms of relations of force, objective situations, etc. – one does not take power in a period of crisis (which would be the same as the management of the crisis of capital, but we know that capital is only waiting for this administrative relief, cf. Sanguinetti). But certainly this is nonsense because a resolved crisis would not allow for the possibility of a revolutionary 'relief'.

Once again another tactical explanation, but more complex this time: if the party takes power, it finds itself in a dilemma or, on the other hand, it falls into a total reformism in order to preserve its electorate – and in this perspective it loses ground to the socialists (more generally, in the reformist perspective, the Left is losing in relation to the Right, which makes it even better); or, rather, it is summoned to assure its revolutionary perspectives, and it is immediately swept aside. Caught between these two sides, the party's only choice is to keep itself inside the line of power, where it can look like it wants to win and thereby save its image without actually doing anything in order to escape this shadow, in the trial of the reality of power, where it loses without reprieve. It simultaneously lets the Right continually play on the imminence of a communist victory in order to maintain its power by inertia. This is how the political tourniquet works, an endless scenario where the bets are placed and where the same cards are suddenly re-dealt.

Nevertheless, this doesn't explain yet why the communists are incapable of playing the game of politics, that is to say, to politically assume a dissociation of means and ends – the principle of politics where power is the end and anything else is the means; they are obsessed by the means and have lost sight of the ends; they are obsessed by progressive results, the slow progression of the masses, the grasping of historical consciousness, etc.; they no longer believe in any of that, and through force of will, following a good super-Kantian ethic, homogenize the means and the ends in order to make power itself a means, but they have lost the scope to take it. They have been divested of all political violence – because of this they are everywhere and always victims, and they hold on to only this miserabilist myth of the masses dominated by an exploitative power. This is the only substance of all of their discourse; a lamentable and plaintive recrimination addressing itself to whose pity, to what instance of justice, to which god who will avenge them on capital?

The communists perhaps never really had a taste for power.[1] *Insofar as they were communists*, they never had a taste for anything other than *bureaucratic domination* – which is different from the exercise of politics, and is nothing but a caricature of it.

Nevertheless Stalinism is still accused of political violence, because it exceeded the pure and simple *use value* of history, the masses, labour, and the social. There is still something of an absurd imperium, let loose beyond a rational finality of the social (André Glucksmann's error with respect to the terrorist logic of the Stalinist camps, 'labour' camps as opposed to the Nazi extermination camps, and which would be a more accomplished model of domination). Perhaps this is the secret of the communists' failure, of their complex political impotence: since Stalin and his death they have increasingly *aligned themselves on the basis of use value* through a naïve belief in a possible transparency of history and the social, through the elimination all other dimensions except that of a sane management of things, by which they have fallen into an incredible *morality* typical of the best days of Christianity. Having lost the immoral and excessive aspects of the idea of revolution, which would have challenged capital on the field of its virulence (and not on that of its presumed rationality), this is a much poorer revolution than one that might have been, because it is unable to manage the nation, only seek the relief of capital. In its 'savage' ethic, capital itself never considered use value, nor the social's proper use – it pursued the demented enterprise, without limits, of abolishing the symbolic universe in an ever greater indifference and an endless circulation accelerated by value.

Capital is just that: the limitless rule of exchange value. At the symbolic and ritualistic levels capital doesn't oppose a rational order of interest, profit, production, or work, in short an order of positive finalities. It imposes a disconnection, a deterritorialization of all things, an excessive extension of value, an equally irrational order of investment *at all costs* (the contrary of rational calculation according to Weber). Capitalism's rationality is nonsense: capital is a challenge to the natural order of value, a challenge that knows no limits. It foresees the triumph of (exchange) value at all costs, and its axiom isn't production but investment. Everything must be gambled, put at stake. The true capitalist does not thesaurize, enjoy or consume; his productivity is an endless spiral, he converts all production to an ulterior productivity – without regard for needs, for human and social ends. That, at least, is the nature of the immoral or measureless capitalism that dominated from the eighteenth century to the start of the twentieth century.

Marxism is nothing but the degraded form. Socialism is not the dialectically superior form of capital; it is nothing but the degraded, banalized form of the social, the form *moralized* by political economy (itself reduced by Marx to its *critical* dimension, and having thus lost its irrational and ascetic dimension which Weber highlights in his *Protestant Ethic*), and the political economy itself entirely *moralized by use value*.

All *political* (and not just economic) good conscience found refuge in use value. The process must be reconsidered under a harsher light than at the level of objects and goods. This time it must occur at the level of the social as a whole because this time it is the use value of the social that is at stake, *the social as use value*.

The dialectical rainbow that long shone on the Marxist notion of commodities and the sacred horizon of value has dissolved, and we can now see, in its shining fragments, of what it consisted: not only is use value nothing, it functions as the codpiece of political economy (what Marx, it must be noted, had subtly pointed out, but no one who speaks for him has since noticed, is that since all of socialism and the whole idea of revolution and the end of political economy are governed by the triumph of use value over exchange value, and the end of commodity alienation, the universe is transfigured by use value, from that of objects to that of, sexually speaking, one's own body and, to each, the image of one's proper 'needs'), but it is worse than that: *it is the degraded form of exchange value*. It is the completely disenchanted form of the economy, the neuter, abolished phase of utility, which brings to a close the delirious, endless process of commodity exchange, of the instantiations of all things in the sublime form of money (a process that, as we know, impassions *everyone* collectively, whereas use, function, and need, etc., simply 'interest' each of us in an eternal resigned manner in isolation). When an object, a being or an idea has found its use value (its function etc.), it is finished, it leads to total entropy. Use value is like heat in the second law of thermodynamics: THE LOWEST FORM OF ENERGY.

The communists believe in the use value of work, the social, matter (their materialism), and history. They believe in the 'reality' of the social, struggles, classes, who knows what else? They believe everything, they want to believe in everything this is their profound morality. This is what robs them of all of their capacity for politics.

Yet they no longer believe in the sacred horizon of appearances – the revolution wants to put an end to appearances – but only in the restricted horizon of reality. They believe in the management of things and in an empirical revolution that will follow over the course of time. They believe in the coherence and the continuity of time. Every aspect of excess, immorality, and the seduction and simulation that constitute politics escapes them. This is what makes them foolish, profoundly foolish, profoundly riveted to their bureaucratic mentality. It is what, more concretely, makes them ill-suited to assume or to maintain power. With a certain municipal grin and the provincial roundness of middle-class technicians (the 'middle classes' result from the historical domestication and degradation by use value), they have become administrators of the use value of life. It is at the level of the atrocity of exchange value and its generalized system that the 'proletariat' fought, that is to say, the revolutionary level of capital, and playing to death against it their proper inhumanity of exchange value. Today, by contrast, everything takes the form of infantile pleas for ever greater use value, and this, this is the ideology of the middle class. Socialism and communism express the degradation of the dominant values of capital and the collapse of the political game.

In order to become pure and simple theoreticians and practitioners of the *proper use of the social* through the proper use of political economy, the communists have fallen even lower than capital and are only capable of presiding over the management of the most degraded form of the law of value.

The dialectic is definitively over. The grand Marxist promise has ended. 'The condition of the liberation of the working class is the liquidation of all class, just as the liberation of the Third Estate [of the bourgeois order] was the liquidation of all states'.

This isn't true, because the dialectic is over – or, rather, this is the infantile fantasy of Marxist theory – it never stopped being on the side of capitalism. And what becomes clear, because the communists' taking power is impossible thanks to their phobia of power, is the proletariat's historical inability to accomplish that which the bourgeoisie had in its time: revolution.

When the bourgeoisie put an end to the feudal order, it actually subverted one total order and code of social relations (birth, honour, hierarchy) in order to substitute another (production, economy, rationality, progress). And it is because it lives as a *class* (not as an *order* or an *estate*: 'Third Estate' is a term that we have assigned it) – that is to say, as something that is radically new, a radically new concept of the social relation – that it could disrupt the order of caste.

The proletariat does not posses anything to radically oppose to the order of a class society. Contrary to the bourgeoisie, which plays its part (the economy) by imposing its code, the 'proletariat' pretends to liberate itself in the name of production, that is to say, the terms in whose name the bourgeoisie *liberated* itself as a class would be the same as those in which the proletariat would *negate* itself as a class! Misdeeds of the dialectic, with which the bourgeoisie infected the proletariat. The bourgeoisie does not 'dialectically surpass' the feudal order; it substitutes for it an unprecedented order of value – the economy, production, class as an antagonistic code lacking common measure with the feudal code. And its true strategy is to trap the proletariat in the *status* of class, more accurately the *struggle* of classes – why not? – because class is a code and the bourgeoisie has the monopoly: the bourgeoisie is the only class in the world – if it has succeeded in leading the proletariat to recognize itself as a class, even if *it is in order to negate itself as such*, it means that it has won.

The genuine relief that would assure (that has occasionally been assured) the communists and the Left is not the one that Sanguinetti announced, in order to denounce, in his *True Report*. It is much more gloomy and more subtle: *the communists will one day take power in order to hide the fact that it no longer exists*. It will therefore not consist of a subversion of capital, nor a revolution of capital on itself, but quite simply a political involution, a reabsorption of the political and of all political violence in a society devoted to the exclusive game of mass simulation.

b. September 1977. Castrated on his Wedding Night

The Left is Poulidor: he vigorously pedals towards power, the crowds cheer wildly, and at the moment of triumph he falls back into second place, into the shadows, into the opposition's corner. Or, rather, the Left is Eurydice: as soon as power turns to seize her, she returns to Hades, a virgin martyr shared amongst the shades of tyrants.

A cyclical, mythological truce. Is the disappointment of 23 September a matter of political failure or is it due to the fact that we have been robbed of all political expiry dates? Even the disarray of the Right is an interesting symptom; its incapacity to exploit what should, for it, be a victory but is not one, for what is at play in the anticipated scenario of the victory and decomposition of the Left is precisely *anticipation*, the precession of the scenario of the end of history, and this is just as deadly for the Right as for the Left, because it means the end of all strategic perspectives. The entire political class is laid low by this reversion of politics into simulation, in the face of which neither the presiding forces nor the silent masses can do anything because, despite all the manipulation, no one can be said to master the process of simulation (something else perhaps occurs at the level of the 'silent masses').

Both the Left and the Right accuse each other of appearing to disunite in order to reunite at the appropriate moment, that is to say, of having a strategy. This is but a trick to amuse the crowds. In reality, the Right and the Left, *taken together*, work with each other on the expression of their differences and in the preservation of the model of political simulation, and this collusion dominates their respective strategies from afar. Beyond this there are no real strategies in this system of simulated disagreement and dissuasion (which is also that of pacific coexistence at a global level), but a sort of destiny that absorbs us all, the destiny of the ineluctable production of the social, and of dissuasion by the social (and we all claim the production of the social to be an irreversible ideal, if only to oppose it). In this system, with its tactical division of labour, the defection of one of the parties (today the Left) is a sort of betrayal, a low-blow, an *acte manqué*, because it leads to a disinvestment in politics – so much energy escaping the sphere of absorption of the social, and this means a loss for all. Clearly the Left is conducting itself poorly. It plays at the fantasy of tearing itself apart over nothing, while its true role, that which it cannot escape, is to be a solid and trustworthy partner in the political balancing act with the Right, a good pole for the transmission of the social's electricity (and here one recovers the conjunction of soviets and electricity in the definition of socialism, like that of the umbrella and the sewing machine on the operating table).

On the other hand, one might say (and what is amusing about this story is that all hypotheses are simultaneously possible, and that this precisely is what today defines the political [or its end]: the succession of all hypotheses as in a state of weightlessness where none annuls another, the cyclical overlaying and inter-ference of all models – but it is just this *anti-gravitation*, this indetermination, that is exciting because it puts an end to all political strategy and all political ration-ality) that if the problem of the coming to power of the Left as a sort of epider-mal turn of the universal to 'socialism' is occurring, to one degree or another, throughout the world, it is not, or is no longer, the traditional vicissitudes of a Right that, having been worn out by the exercise of power, surrenders it to the Left in order that the latter serve as the relief and momentary transmission belt for the 'dominant class'. The Left as the historical prosthesis of the Right (which is not false either). This is the hypothesis that is still at the heart of Sanguinetti's book on the best means to save capital in Italy.

But if today we admit that the fundamental question is no longer that of capi-tal, but that of the social, and that the only means of the social's regeneration of its accelerated production is the discourse of crisis, then we would expect that the Left, because it is born of and nourished by critical thought, will impose itself on power as the most credible spokesperson, the most coherent symbol, and most faithful mirror of the crisis. It will claim power no longer in order to resolve a real crisis (such a crisis doesn't exist), but in order to manage the *discourse* of crisis, the critical phase of capital, which will be endless because it is that of the social.

If there is something to be retained from Marx it is this: capital produces the social, it is its essential production, its 'historical function'. And the great moments of the social, the convolutions and revolutions, coincide with capital's ascending phase. When the objective determinations of capital lose their force, the social will not overcome capital according to some dialectical movement. The social, too, will collapse, even as a moribund Real corresponds to an anaemic Imaginary. This is what we are witnessing today: the Left dying of the same causes as power.

But we can also say (always these 'reversible' hypotheses) that the Right always runs the risk, after a certain time in power, of stagnation, of an involu-tion of the social (the mass participation etc.). The only solution is a reinjection, an overdose of political simulation in the agonizing social body. Revolution in homeopathic doses, distilled by the Left, which thus acts as a relay in the production of the social, just like the unions asserted themselves by assuring the relief of capital in the socialization of work. Do they owe their success to anything else?

The paradox of this advent of socialism and of the Left is that it arrives *too late*, when the process of socialization, after the violent ascending phases of capitalist socialization, is already in decline, when the social resigns itself to its own loss. The Left never attains 'power' except to manage its own resignation, the slow dis-aggregation, reabsorption, involution, and implosion of the social – it is this we call socialism. Thus the unions do not obtain uncontested management over the sphere of work, except when the process of work, by its own generalization, loses its historical virulence and gets mired in the writing of its own representation.

But is this kind of socialism capable of ending our grief at the loss of the social? Certainly not: it can only multiply the signs of the social and simulate the social to death. In which case, as is usual with all failed mourning, we can pre-dict that we will plunge into melancholy.

The most interesting thing about the present episode is the precession of the scenario before the Real. A kind of premature ejaculation (everything is played and played out six months before the elections) that is equivalent to a temporal castration, a rupture in the scansion of the event which always underlies an unforeseeable conjunction and a minimal moment of uncertainty. May '68 had a high degree of factuality, being neither foreseen, nor a model for future epi-sodes. Here it is completely the opposite: about-faces, surprises, ruptures; it's all a Punchinello script, preformed deliberately by old politicos, a false, premature event which takes away from what was already no more than a pseudo-event: the elections and the minimal political suspense that still held. This is the result of a system of calculated programming and de-programming, a system of dissuasion where even the Real no longer has the opportunity to produce itself.

Independently of the motives and machinations of each of the actors in this vaudeville, what disgusts us all – and about which we can do nothing – is the effacing of the few opportunities, the minimal charm, the Real, the event's real-ity principle, still held. The Real will no longer happen, the relations of force that it could have unleashed are still-born; only the phantom of the silent majority still hovers over this desert, bowing in advance before the reckoning of the ballot-boxes whose results matter even less than an episode from a past life, since the curtain has already fallen.

And the CP [Communist Party] will, nonetheless, be considered the most responsible in this affair (even though simulation's devastation lies far beyond its capacities) because it contributed the most to the secularization of this indiffer-ence, to this general distaste for politics to the benefit of a disciplined manage-ment, and economistic vision, the pure transparency of the social. In this fury to bring about the social in its purity, as a pure abstraction, the zero-degree of politi-cal energy, in its rage for a pure and simple management of the social, the CP has had every opportunity because it is the only 'homogeneous' social apparatus. But just this homogeneity could itself be no more than an effect of the apparatus, and the social itself, once reduced to the degree zero, could well implode brusquely under the buttocks.

The absurdity of a 'government pact', as if power were no more than a means to apply a programme. It implies such scorn for power, such a misunderstanding of politics, that the latter, in some sense, takes its revenge, for the unfitness for political sovereignty is closely related to this impoverished concept of power as use value. By dint of analysing the State as the executive gear-wheels of the 'dominant class', the communists have denied themselves the energy to take it over (let alone to abolish it!). Power as a *form*, whose contents are unpredictable, and whose stakes can be reversed, the logic of the political being capable of leading the man or the class in power to undermine its own basis or objectives – this is what must be avoided at all costs. There is only one solution: programming. The political must be neutralized in advance via economic and social rationality. The form must obey only its anterior content, just as the real event must be no more than an echo of a calculated script. The same dissuasion, same contraception, same deception.

The reason that the masses, in whom no doubt an incurable capacity for political hallucination still resides, hoped for a 'victory of the Left': unforeseen tomorrows. And this is what they must be discouraged from, before it is too late, by chaining them to a programmatic logic. All programmes are dissuasive because they arm themselves against the future. What is more, they offer the possibility of making and unmaking situations before they take place. One can update them indefinitely without the risk of actualizing them; one can expend an insane amount of energy on them which would otherwise be quite threatening. It is the model raised to the power of preventative jurisdiction for an entire society. The blackmail of the programme can be substituted for all repression. Between the hard technologies of persuasion and forced socialization and the soft technologies of pure dissuasion, the programme represents the bastard form of modernist social bureaucracies.

The panic at the central committee must have been serious towards the beginning of summer in anticipation of victory. However, can we assume that the dissuasion operation had already been set up since the presidential elections, once it was clear that the fifty/fifty threshold was going to be surpassed and the investiture inevitable? At that moment, a great surge of hope as a prelude to the baptism of power – but it was *too early*, much too early, as one sells the bear's fur out of *fear* of killing it, as one imagines the devil in order to make him back away – and simultaneously, the finalizing of the scenario of dissuasion, of demobilization, and let-down. But this is the whole history of the CP: an equal amount of energy is employed to mobilize the 'masses' and then demobilize them, resulting in a zero-sum game. This is the social's great game, to cycle and recycle the masses, to accelerate the cycle and break it, stimulation and inertia – such was the orbit of China's cultural revolution – with its high points of dissuasion ('45: disarm! – '48: know how to end a strike – '68: general strike and elections and, this time, rupture of the Union of the Left). We will never adequately evaluate the historical role of the CP as a dissuasion machine, a machine for the futile, and cyclical combustion of energy. And what remains? Precisely the social, the social as cumulative waste, as growing excretion, as what remains from all failed revolutions, the fallout, the inert mass that covers everything in accordance with an abstraction that sees its full realization in socialism. Those famous social conquests, which, for a century, have constituted the entire ideology of the Left, are naught but the phases of this growing neutralization.

The funniest thing is that the CP and Marchais still take themselves for historical bogies, proclaiming in a bogus manner: 'But of course we want power!' They who spent twenty years protesting in their innocence that 'No we don't want power!' in order to gain acceptance into political entente – now the irony is that they are suspected of not wanting it. Never will there be a more beautiful example of an apparatus that has made a mockery of itself, but, deep down, everyone applauds this role because they all need the CP as it has become with its political emasculation, strutting, arrogant, buffoonish, vainglorious peacock, chauvinist, managerial – incarnating the visible face of revolution, the ever-visible face of a revolution endlessly gravitating around the orbit of capital.

But all the other parties, and undoubtedly we too, inwardly, still magnify it excessively in the disarray that comes with imagining its disappearance. It is still the last great vestige of a superseded era of the political. And therein lies its force, in blackmail and nostalgia. And its current triumph is to block the situation with an archaic problematic (nationalizations, national defence, the standard of living of the labouring masses) in which, in its best moments, it does not itself believe. The CP only made sense from the perspective of the dictatorship of the proletariat. Today it finds itself before the inertia of the masses, an inertial force which undoubtedly contains a new violence – but in the face of the social's dissolution, of this diffuse, unintelligible solution that the social, like the political, has become, the CP, like so many others, is at a loss.

Still we must try to understand. It is not easy, in a society rapidly evolving towards soft technologies (including those that relate to power), to maintain a hard ideology and apparatus. Monopoly, centralization, programme planning, bureaucracy, nuclear defence – the CP remains the last great adversary of a sociality made supple, cool, self-managing, ecological, contactual (and no longer contractual). Against the 'psy' society, with its blend of porno, libido, and schizo, the party remains on the side of the disciplinary society, that of the asylum, the prison and the apparatus, still entirely within panoptic space – thus tending to Stalinism, but without Stalinism's political violence – a Stalinism on cruise, decked out in New Age tinsel that makes it looks like a drag queen.

To be sure, the fluid, tactile, tactical, and psychedelic society towards which we are moving, the era of soft technologies, is no less ferocious than that of hard technologies; and one might even think, before the disquieting strangeness of simulation, that one misses the dictatorship of the proletariat, which was a clear, vigorous concept (even if it was a dictatorship exercised *over* the proletariat – a matter of little importance for the utopian transparency of the concept: even in the ambiguity of its genitive case, it was a strong concept). Today there is no longer any proletariat exercising a violent dictatorship over itself through the mediation of a despot; this is still the political spirit of the totalitarian State, with its tendency toward extermination, whose extreme form is the camps, with the despot's insane dream of *putting an end to his own people* (in 1945 Hitler condemned the German people to death). There is no longer anything but the fluid, silent masses, the variable equation of multiple surveys, the object of perpetual tests which, like an acid, dissolve the masses. To test, survey, contact, solicit, inform – this is a bacterial tactic, a virulent tactic whereby the social ends with infinitesimal dissuasion, wherein it no longer even has time to crystallize. Violence formerly crystallized the social, forcefully giving birth to an antagonistic social energy. This is still the demiurge of Stalinism. Today we are guided by a soft semiurgy.

The question remains to be posed of possible resistance to this invasive tactility, of the possible reversal of simulation on the very basis of the social's death, in addition to the problem of a 'desocialized' nebula and the new processes of implosion that result. But, to the soft technologies, the CP opposes only the artificial maintenance of a social apparatus of 'the mass' and an archaic ideology of 'mobilization' while everything is already much more mobile than it thinks. Everything circulates uncontrollably, *including the CP itself*, which, like everyone else and in spite of itself, moves tactically without any strategy, or any real social or historical system of references (except those long recycled), but desperately feigning the contrary: that is, solid infrastructures and irreducible finalities. But this archaic resistance itself serves, once more, as a functional bogy for the society of tolerance, an ideological sanctuary for the conservation of the masses.

The CP has an idea of the masses, of the economy, the polity, and revolutions that is just as backwards as that which it always had of culture, which it always conceived of as bourgeois decorative realism and Leftist scientific objectivism. It is the doctrine of the figurative social, that is to say, the political equivalent of figurative realism in painting. All of the revolutions that have taken place since the eighteenth century in form, space, and colour have remained a dead letter relative to particularly revolutionary politics which remain set on the 'historical' principles of truth, reality, and rationality. Not only is there no equivalent in the political sphere to the deconstruction of the object in painting, to abstraction (the deconstruction of political space, the subject of history or the class referent), but up to now there has been no equivalent of the new spiral leading to hyper-realism, the hyper-simulation of the Real, the geared-down game of abyssal representation. Is there nowhere any idea or glimmer in the heads of politicians that all their energy and all their discourses might have become akin to hyper-realist performances, that is, hyper-representative of an unobtainable reality?

A table is always what it is, but it no longer makes sense to represent it 'such as it is'.

A commodity is still what it is (though Marx had already demonstrated that it was no longer what it was), but it no longer makes sense to talk about its use value nor, no doubt, about its exchange value, which still comes under the representative space of the commodity.

Power is still what it is, but it no longer makes sense to speak about what it represents, nor to represent it as 'real'.

The real itself is what it is, but it no longer makes sense to think or reflect upon it as such.

The CP, like the real, like the social, is still what it is, but it is no doubt precisely no more than that: that is, it has exhausted itself in its own likeness. Hyper.

Because at bottom it is all the same (it is not a matter of coming to terms with a loss for the latter still implies the referent of melancholy, and still leads, like the psychoanalytic transference, to a solution: the death implied by such mourning is still a real psychic event and integral to its 'history'). It is the same as the deconstruction, abstraction, and hyperrealization that has taken place in the domain of visual representation and sensorial perception. Without anyone helping it, it also took place in the political, economic, and social spheres. And the ever-expanding reach of the social has long since been that of a dead or hyper-real sociality, just as the ever-expanding reach of work is no more than that of dead work, obsessive signs of the now terminated case against work, just as the reach of sex is only that of the sexual model, hyper-realized in the omnipresent signs of liberation, in the inevitable, orgasmic scripts, in desire's endless finality.

We are very far from all the discourses of this world, which, from Left to Right, are immersed in political realism. But perhaps this realist blindness only touches what should be called the 'political class', who alone believe in politics and political representation, just as advertisers are the only ones who believe in advertising.

The social, the idea of the social, the political and the idea of the political, have no doubt always been held by only a minority. Instead of conceiving the social as a sort of original condition, a factual state that encompasses everything else, or an *a priori* transcendental given not unlike time and space (but precisely, time and space have since been relativized as a code which the social has not – on the contrary, its naturalism has been reinforced: everything has become social, we bathe in it as in a maternal placenta, socialism has crowned it by inscribing it as a future set of ideals – and everyone does sociology to death; we explore the least incidents, the smallest nuances of the social without questioning the axiom of the social itself), we need to ask: who produced the social, who determined this discourse, who deployed its code, stirred up this universal simulation? Was it not a certain technical, rationalizing, and humanist cultural intelligentsia who found in the social the means to think everything and enframe it within a universal concept (perhaps the only one) which gradually discovered a grandiose referent: the silent masses from which the social's essence appears to emerge and its inexhaustible energy radiate? But have we considered that most of the time neither these individuals nor the masses experience the social, live as social, that is to say, within that perspectival, rational, and panoptic space within which the social and its discourse think themselves?

There are societies without the social, just as there are societies without writing. This only seems absurd because the terms themselves are absurd – if they are no longer societies, what are they? Groups, ethnicities, categories: we fall back into the same terminology – the distortion between the hypothesis and the discourse is irreparable. Without referring to other 'societies', how can one designate, here and now, what in the 'masses' (who are supposed to incarnate the indifferentiation and generality of the social) lives beneath, beyond or outside of the social and what is brewing at this level? How do we designate this non-sense, this unnameable remainder? It is not a matter of anarchy, asociality, or desocialization, but a profound and radical indifference to the *relation* and *determination* of the social as a code and as an *a priori* hegemonic system. It is not a matter of lapses, gaps, or accidents of the social, nor of those who in their singularity resist it (the insane, drug-users, homosexuals) – the latter are in fact the experimental categories of the social and will one day be assigned a place in a thoroughgoing sociality. It consists of something which is, precisely, not a remainder, excess or exception, but massive, banal, and indistinct, something more powerful than the social, which doesn't transgress it, but which simply does not know about laws or principles. Something that evades representation, since the social and the political are of the domain of representation and the law. What do we know about this massive, but not passive, indifference, of this challenge by inertia at the very heart of manipulation? What do we know about this zone where the social, which is meaning, has perhaps never happened?

c. January–April 1978. Lament for a Defunct Left

i. What makes Marchais laugh?   30 January. What gives him this air of victory, this fantastic insolence, when everyone else is so unhappy? This kind of joy can only come from the singular exaltation of the certainty of losing while showing all the inverse signs of a resolute will to succeed. It can only be the malign joy of having to refuse power when we don't want it and taking advantage of this refusal in order to maintain a position of oppositional force. The joy of the assured manipulation where adversaries are mobilized in spite of themselves for the realization of your own objectives. A sarcastic joy, the joy of dressing up in the garb of one's artificial ghetto, a negative but profound joy because it comes from the depths of political abjection, born of the radical resignation of all political will or strategy and the exhaustion of one's force in this contrary manipulation. A fascinating example of a party that would gather all its energies to discourage a potential majority from bringing it to power. *Se nier en tant que telle* – the famous historical countersign of the proletariat – never realized, since the concept and the reality of 'class' will have been volatilized even before being able to surpass it 'as such', from which the dismissal *sine die* of the revolution derives; otherwise fully realized by the party itself insofar as it is a political apparatus, and no longer assumes any position of power than one internal to its own apparatus, secreting no more than the minimal, homeostatic, doses of power necessary for the regulation of the apparatus, devoting all of its energies to maintaining and reinforcing a potential that will never again be put into play. Sophistication of the means to the exclusion of ends, inflation of the organization, deflation of the political stakes and the political will: this is at bottom an ecological practice. The CP marches to the tune of savings, to the economy, to self-sufficiency. It unconsciously answers to the question: how can power be economized when nothing, or so little, remains? How can a rare resource that is on the way to disappearance be economized? How can the political be made to work with the least cost, with the minimum of investment, risks, and expirations – ultimately: how can the illusion of a political will to power be given, how can the political stake be escaped without destroying one's own reality principle? A nice programme for future generations, destined, there as elsewhere, to manage residues and compensate for shortcomings (political exhaustion as raw materials)!

Moreover, it is already on this basis that the CP prospers and recruits among the young. The CP is a structure that receives all of the political *disoccupati*. Antidepressant, anti-melancholic, distributor of a hormonal politics, it still constitutes a haven of the lures of the social for all who will not have been spoiled by history. It manages political unemployment like the national employment office manages unemployment. It is not therefore ready to disappear because there is every indication that the orphans of the political will grow in number in the future. It stands facing an eternity because it expends its force in this disaffection. Its interest in this inertial force and in the neutralization of the political is the same as Capital might have in the neutralization of productive forces by the inertial force of the 'reserve army' of the unemployed.

Here the CP wins across the board. But who knows if the trap that it sets for an entire political society will not fail, and if, in the March elections, we will not have an unprecedented development: the victory of the Left in spite of all the CP's desperate efforts? The Left seems to be ineluctably led towards the majority by a sort of secret irony. The transhistorical irony of the masses carrying the apparatuses of the Left to power *despite themselves*.

Is there an objective law (a kind of machine that has marched alongside history), a law of inertia, that from now on sides with the Left, while up until this point it worked for the Right? This law of inertia articulates itself as the law of involution towards socialism – the Left acceding to the empty place of the political and filling up the void of the political by the effective monotony of the social and the management of the social – all the better to manage the 'dereliction of the political' (Hannah Arendt) and assuming power to take, as usual, the responsibility of sacrifices (cf. the declarations of Lama and the Italian CGIL [Confederazione Generale Italiana del Lavoro].[2]

The indispensable hypothesis is that the CP would have understood this and at the same time refused it – but this is a useless dream.

The sort of challenge presented to the Left, and the CP in particular, by the masses who will elect it, despite its lack of unity, is more stimulating – by what will to see, 'just to see', as in poker? Perhaps without hoping for something deep-down, but inexorably executing the kind of promise that had been made to them. An astonishing return of the base against the bad political will of the apparatuses: the forces to play with, to perhaps push to catastrophe in an inextricable mixture of historical nostalgia and the anticipated disillusion in the possible consequences. Come what may: the scenario of the Left must come to pass. It must be seen – for the spectacle, for the honour, for the prestige, for a laugh?

All social 'classes' share this itching, the itching of the Left, even if their ideology prohibits it. Aside from the interest the Right might have in relieving itself of power (but it does not seem ready to set in motion or stage its own death with the intelligence that de Gaulle did through the 1969 referendum), everyone waits for this development because it inscribes itself in the *obliged* arrangement of elements in the political sphere. It is effectively no longer a question of choice: the leap must be made, even the challenge presented by statistics must be raised – 53 per cent: the masses, since they are caught like skin by polls and will not believe that statistics are ridiculous and refuse to give them credit. The Left as well can only bow before the power of the masses – this is the aleatory power of statistics.

5 February. This is why the CP also desperately resorts to the statistical cut-off: in order to take its share of power it demands that it obtain 25 per cent of the vote. A surrealist ultimatum: to whom is it addressed? The other parties? Do they prefer that no one would be able to retroactively cede their votes – on what basis? Is this challenge launched to the anonymous electorate, the silent majority? 'If you want the Left in power you must therefore accomplish a statistical miracle'. This challenge is presented to the masses: the cut-off is placed too high to be surmounted (in fact this challenge is nothing but the one the CP presents to its own 'masses'; a challenge to disobey it, to go elsewhere and be illegally represented by others).

In any case, when the cut-off is surpassed the CP will nevertheless give up, having firmly decided that it does not need to submit to the test of power. The only thing it wants is to inflate its numbers so that it can reinforce its ideological blackmail: we are defrauded, we are barred from power! This is an ideal situation for the CP insofar as it would be an opposition unjustly deprived of its rights – *the triumphal position of ressentiment*. The party must continue to be separated from power in order for this blackmail to succeed. This simple equation dictates its entire strategy – but a form of unexpected challenge threatens to unravel it! You want power? Well, then, you will have it! The masses tear down apparatuses in a Pyrrhic victory, calling on them to go to the limit of their so-called reason, and thus tear down the entire system of representation in a suicidal culture.

All parties, all of the political forces, see themselves doubled – no longer on the Left, that was too easy – by a transpolitical necessity of spectacle and game doubled by a provocative inertia that none of them can control!

Through programming and over-programming the CP hoped to finally evade power. And there are the masses, cursing the programme, which they, deep down, suspect of contradiction and sophistries, who risk bringing them to power anyway. Power *without* the programme, while the operative word was: the programme against power. This is a singular reversal.

The situation is no less scabrous for the SP [Socialist Party], because if it truly wants power it is again in terms of the idealism of a programme. Thousands of socialist intellectuals are in the process of elaborating, in the most complete *realist* illusion of politics, all of the *solutions* following March '78, from the atomic dissuasion right up to the pursuit of the Brussels negotiations on the Lomé accords, and it led to their adoption during the reunion of the CNUCED [Conférence de Nations Unies sur le Commerce et le Développement] held in Geneva before summer. Idealists to the core, naïve to their fingertips, they think that power is made from concrete courageous decisions, and behind this programmatic good faith they are already in Allende's skin, committed to suicide. Mitterrand always had the head of a suicide victim (Giscard only has the distinguished head of someone who has been guillotined). In any case, the SP will find itself in a contrary position as well, because if elected by the masses it is not because of a programme, but *in order to see it* in power.

The misunderstanding is complete, which accounts for the discreet charm of the elections. Properly political power, which is avoided by all of the forces present, who are no more than the executrices of a programme, is absorbed by power as spectacle, the only remaining power that distributes the moving masses and statistics – because, let's have no illusions, they will reelect the Right the next time around, but *this is not important* – they want a spectacle, a sign, not a changing society! They want a beautiful spectacle, not a good programme!

They do not want to be 'represented'. They want to watch a representation (they don't even want to represent themselves, self-management hardly moves them). They have had enough of representation as a destiny, in whatever form. They want to take advantage of the spectacle of representation. All of the representatives (parties, unions) make use of the 'social exigency of the masses' to escape politics (and the CP, if it wasn't for its cowardice, has good reason to be suspicious of political power, which no longer exists – or is nothing more than a trap of representation – in order to be confident in the day-to-day administration, the 'municipal' aspect, of the social), but the masses don't want to see it this way: they prefer the spectacle – even the grotesque or derisive one – of politics to the rational administration of the social.

Perhaps the experience of the social scarcely pleases them? Perhaps this historical experiment that was launched in their home, on their backs, is not at all to their liking? Perhaps they do not want to be taken for masses and cornered by historical responsibilities? Perhaps they are fed up with the real and the rational, the concrete and 'objective' problems, even and above all their own? Perhaps they prefer the baroque drama of the end of politics, the absurd charm of the political class that 'negates itself as such', according to the well-known adage, and takes to the streets as in anti-theatre, flattering the masses, inviting the garbage-collectors to the Elysée, being invited to the Elysée, outdoing itself in demagogic baseness – perhaps they prefer all of this to the all-too familiar social experimentation that takes place on their backs?

The masses are not dumb enough to get rid of representation, power, or responsibility – all decayed values, worn out by a long history and which would continue to bear the cost if they were invested in. They are too content to discharge their own 'representatives'. Women use the same trick. We believe that they are defrauded. What nonsense! They unburden themselves of power. Will, responsibility, power, are all foolish, dangerous, and, today, derisive things. It is what the Gods send to the race of men to lose them. The masses, since the earliest mythology and history, have always, through a secret irony, let heroes fall like expiatory victims, while savouring the spectacle of their death. Today nothing has changed, and the strange crack that has appeared in the political playing field bears the trace of this burlesque comedy: the masses condemn those who no longer want power or those who have some left. The silent and ironic efficiency of the aleatory majorities: they had long been subject to the social experiment; today they experiment with the political, or what remains of it, and the very tenets of political class. Turned back against its own defenders, and seemingly against its own interests, the silent majority nevertheless leans towards the Left, towards an obscure goal that is currently not the quality of life, nor the satisfaction of its needs, nor its 'right to the social'.

'The more woman is woman', Nietzsche said, 'the more she defends against any kind of right'. The more the mass is the mass, the more it resists any kind of representation – and the silent majorities do the same.

20 February. The Left will no doubt not win in the end. The CP will not desist the second time around. It will go that far in terms of dissuasion and its will to fail. Nothing will stop its braking and leaking. Without a doubt it will therefore win thanks to the masses and their obscure (and perhaps ironic) will to see the Left at work, put to the test, this divine, elusive Left. But this will have been a fight to the death between an apparatus that is resolved to uncap the political will of the masses and these latter, forcing the apparatuses to play the political game (but no illusions: even if we force them to win, they have sufficient programmatic and bureaucratic means to elude all of the stakes of power). And finally defeated by the ultimate treachery and cunning of the apparatuses (there will be no exception to the historical law according to which the masses are always put down!).

A final nuance: it is possible that the CP so desperately resists the call of its proper masses only because it senses that this will consist of nothing more than pushing it towards catastrophe. Making it play and lose – in order to see, for the spectacle, to exhaust history, empty out the revolutionary hypothesis that for so long had weighed on everyone without revealing itself and which will soon be surpassed without ever having come into being. Is this a temptation to oppose the slow neutralization of politics with an even more violent itinerary, catastrophe, or ordeal? Opposing slow death with violent death?

5 March. There is a new episode in the CP's strategy of dissuasion. Calculating that the refusal to desist would have a disastrous psychological effect, it chose another route: a communist scarecrow. Through an about-face with respect to its previous position, which was to refuse to assume power if it didn't take 25 per cent of the votes (statistical blackmail), today it acts as if it fiercely wants its share of power, a *proportional* share of the ministerial seats. An equally incongruous demand, a foundationless Tartarinade made to scare everyone, one without any other real will than to drive the Left back into failure. This tactic would, without a doubt, be more effective. Since the rupture of the Union wouldn't make the polls vacillate, the following absolute weapon remained for the CP: resuscitate anti-communism, the image of the knife between the teeth, the one that even the Right was no longer able to make work in the conscience of the masses. The CP thus quite gently substituted itself for the lapsing Right in order to block itself off from the route to power.

But what could very well make it act this way? Where is the mystery? Where does its unshakeable resolve come from concerning dissuasion? What malevolent will, what secret strategy, animates it? Don't try to interrogate it: there isn't one – if not those of fully unleavened revolutionary dissuasions, of restraint on its own survival and the discouragement of all else, which belonged to the USSR for the past twenty years (since Cuba, the USSR had checked *all* of the historical revolutionary movements around the globe) and which has more recently belonged to China. There is a certain logic at work in this renunciation of all strategy and in this retreat to an entropic administration of the revolutionary forces. The logic of regression and death.

20 March. The Left has decisively lost, but the communists won some seats. On this occasion they had overtly played on the victory of the Right in order to win a few seats and to move into vacant space that they themselves hollowed out.

Fundamentally speaking, this is no different than in Italy: there also each development allowed the CP to 'push itself' a little bit further ... towards what? Not towards power; it was happy with some technocratic and administrative folding chair conceded by the CDs [Christian Democrats], without demanding anything in return. The CP does not irresistibly ascend to power; it irresistibly occupies a space that was left empty by the reflux and disenchantment of the political sphere. This slow progression is that of the banalization and desertification of civil and political society. Today we no longer know where to find the salt of the earth, but we do know that the CP is the biggest desalinization enterprise. Shame on him to have, with such energy, made the fundamental stupidity necessary for its extension – shame on him to have liquidated the cancerous homeostasis of the social. Marchais mouth: hilarious meta-figure of foolishness and the death drive. A histrionic mouth, exacerbated by burlesque demagogy and by the blackmail of vulgarity that everyone accepts and apparently suffers like a kind of initiation to the future society.

The CP leads to the beatitude of historical compromise: the system must, in effect, tends towards zero without violent development, slowly, progressively, and with a calculated destruction so that the whole of history finishes with a compromise.

The end of history and the political could have been something other than a compromise, it could have constituted a violent and transformative hyper-event, and implosion with incalculable consequences. There are retractions, spoilings, dissolvings that are like revolutions. And those are the big representative political and historical systems; the dissolving of the reality principle itself, and of the principle of sociality, could open onto an unknown conflagration. But the CP is there to prevent the system from dying a violent death. It is a meta-stabilizing brake; it is the historical compromise not with the Right (regardless which Right) but with history itself, given that history does not even have an end. Thus religion, or its successors, succeeded in removing its impact to the event of the death of God, and to distil the consequences in homeopathic doses.

The Italians at least produced the Red Brigades at the same time as the historical compromise. Produced the violent antidote of the slow putrefaction of compromise. What will happen to it? Perhaps Italy is the only society that decomposes in a violent, derisory, and imaginative way. We are still far from this.

ii. What makes Althusser write? We ask ourselves what makes Marchais laugh. Althusser asks: what can no longer endure in the Communist Party?[3] What can no longer endure is quite simply what has endured for fifty years, and whose ritual denunciation marks the annals of the party. Like always, it aims at the restitution of the transparency of the party, a dialectic of the base and the summit (which was never historical), a dialectic of practice and of theory (which has never been philosophical). Nothing new: the anti-Stalinist incantation, which is even more mystifying than the Stalinism of the apparatus.

This address immediately made itself into a kind of event, and everyone greatly rejoiced as if it were a statement of truth. Everyone, that is, but the one who had the greatest reason to rejoice: the CP itself, because the event has nothing historical about it except a kind of bewildering complicity that ties Althusser the accuser with the accused CP, and the total mystification that followed.

The truth is that the CP must be saved: this is the categorical imperative of the entire political class, or rather French society as a whole. The only strong structure upon which the illusion of the political and the social can still hold, and therefore the possibility of making the masses gravitate around the two dead stars, the CP must be saved and resuscitated at all costs. It has been a long time since it ceased to incarnate the threat of seizing power or a subversion of order, but everyone needs the idea, this phantasm of a party (and therein lies its force), otherwise it is the entire political order that falls into disaffection; it is the social, not simply the social order but the social as a whole, that dissolves by brutal desimulation. The CP is the last guarantee of a political and social stake – that of simulation. This is why its existence, credibility, and legitimacy are taboo from one end of the political scale to the other.

But the CP did well during the last elections. Once again it stopped the shuttlecock of history at the retro-point of a Left opposition that was impotent, nostalgic, and pedalling in semolina, but preserving its historical vocation as relief by saving the imaginary of power on the Left by assuring the reality of power on the Right, and granting all political classes an additional lease of five or six years before being affronted at its radical loss of reality and at the crucial end of the political. All things being equal, it is the same thing in Italy – there the referential in peril is the Italian State, and who is going to save it by its regenerative intervention, towards and against everything? The ICP [Italian Communist Party] going so far as to identify itself with it. (Cf. the delectable episode of Aldo Moro: the ICP substitutes itself for the lapsing State to hold firm and sacrifice the head of State, this is the discreet charm of certain historical situations.) The service that the ICP provides to the Italian State is the same one that Althusser delivers to the CP.

This last risked paying dearly, following the elections, not so much for the eminent service rendered to the Right (understood within the political class, whether it be the Right or Left, and without much importance), but with their political disaffection in general. Because this is what is serious: political disenchantment, the foretaste of death, the dissuasion of all political stakes, spectacle, and preconceived opinions about the future. This profound deception, which was shared by the militants, this division of the imaginary in order to better reign over the real, this mortification, was hidden in the thundering and boastful face of Marchais. If the CP only wanted to defeat the SP at the cost of a common failure, it would still have been a *political* strategy, and certainly, this one or another ... but it is still more honourable than attributing a strategy of 'failure' to the CP. This involves hiding the real reason: to know that the CP, quite beyond the socialists, checkmates *all strategies*, checkmates the unfolding of history, that it has become a force of dissuasion and deception without example, and that all that it has to offer is a *moral*, a *domestic* moral: save the furniture, save the apparatuses, save the State, save the institutions. Certainly no strategy, for strategy is dangerous: a *programme*. No prophecy or adventure: the solidity of institutions is founded on the failure of prophecies. And it must be realized that each political failure is followed by a wave of subscriptions to the party, an eternal object of stupefaction for logical reasons. This is because militancy rests on this kind of disappointed investment. Because we have been frustrated from achieving victory, or a counterfeit or parody of the big night, we are able, *with a stubborn resignation*, to invest in a long-term practice that is even more stubborn than the promise of a new failure. 'We will have them in five years!' As we know, if the kingdom of God were of this world, the Church would not exist.

The CP is therefore right to circle indefinitely around power, like a cat, without wanting to take it, because it only sees *deferred revolution*. Each failure of the revolution, each missed opportunity (but only slightly missed), reinforces it in its being, in the wait, and in the institution in the long term. It likes the elections, and it reassures the silent majority, to the Right, that it will save it from victory and the risks of power. The ideal situation for it is to be just beneath 50 per cent. This allows it to avoid playing alternation (where it would be shaved down by the SP), or revolution (where it would be shaved down by history). This permits it to remain in the reserve of the Left, the reserve of the Republic, the reserve of History, and the reserve of the Revolution. This ghetto where it encloses itself, and about which it gives the impression of complaining, is the only artificial milieu where it can survive. There it can exercise its great, gentle force, its frozen vocation of administration sheltered from power, its vocation as silent oppositional majority.

This is the *truth* of the CP, the unsurpassable truth of the Communist Party. Not only that of its apparatus but that of the apparatus and the militants altogether. The institution as a whole is operational from bottom to top, and in this sense there is a sovereign hypocrisy on Althusser's part in dissociating once again the militant from the apparatus, idealizing one in contrast with the other. What permits him to make this discrimination if not his old philosophic morality and the intention to remake a virtue and a virginity for the party on the back of militants reconsidered and corrected as dissidents of the apparatus? It takes a marvellous candour to simultaneously declare to the militants that they are the salt of the party, but that for the past fifty years they were only capable of being subordinated, manipulated, duped, and violated by the apparatus! This accuses them of historical intelligence and incurable stupidity. This suspects them more than the apparatus itself does.

Marchais is perfectly right to disagree with Althusser: it is true that the militants, in their immense majority, are happy, and that the party, *such as it is*, offers them what they desire. Otherwise they wouldn't remain, or maybe they are just stupid. We will not escape, Althusser will not escape: either the suspicion of fact behind the idealist vision, or the necessity of abandoning one's entire analysis of a conspiracy of the top against the bottom, of a supposed abuse of power and mystification by the apparatus, which always tends in fact to regenerate the party's *essence*. This problem otherwise far surpasses the party and enlists all contemporary social analysis: are the masses nothing more than a herd that is eternally alienated and manipulable to the extreme by a supposed power that instrumentalizes them without the least resistance? Will we decide to analyse the nature of the 'passivity' of the masses and their presumed manipulation? Althusser's whole analysis rests on an ideology of the inverse transparency (always dreamed of, always disappointed) of the militant.

His entire argument comes back to:

- opposing the militant to the apparatus;
- opposing the party to what it should be;
- opposing the party to its own policy.

In short, never taking part in the party such as it is. Heated up by a foreign 'dialectical' negativity (from theory, practices of the base, etc.).

What naïveté other than that of its own 'theoretical exigency' in relation to the party which has long since objectively abolished the old theory/practice distinction in a *circular logic* from the base to the summit. No dialectic: a circularity proper to mass communication. A cool universe without dialectical warmth, but the party has long understood that dialectics is a dish best eaten cold. It only needs, at regular intervals, a hormonal reinjection of 'democracy', 'critical spirit', 'anti-Stalinism', a *homeopathic graft*. No dialectic: homeopathy. It was always the work of oppositional generations, from Sartre in the past, to Althusser today: resuscitate the imaginary of the party by refusing for the thousandth time the Stalinist pathology of the apparatus. In doing so they erase the entire original analysis of an original situation: the liquidation not only of the proletariat and its dictatorship, but of politics itself and all strategy: the liquidation not only of the class struggle, but of the social itself and the party in its social definition. What does the party still represent? Neither the proletariat, nor the class struggle, nor even a veritable relation of forces, it incarnates only the social in its vaguest definition, the floating social that is ours today. Extinguishing itself in its living works and in its historical definition by the drifting of the social, the party is nothing more than low-definition machinery, but of fully unleavened management; no longer metallurgy and bureaucracy in the image of the factory, the specific image of the Stalinist era, but vague and opportunist with a variable geometry, marching much more to manipulation and recycling than to hierarchy and economic management, much more to dissuasion than to intoxication and discipline.

The anti-Stalinist critique of the party is therefore only a mystifying diversion. Stalinism is the cold monster that we show to small children. But Stalinism is no longer the essential problem anywhere, and, moreover, it is not even true that the party is Stalinist – nor 'democratic' from another point of view – it is already something else, also floating, lacking a referent and a strategy (while Stalinism presupposes a strong referent and strategy): evolving structure, in involution or in perdition – the interesting developments that are here offered to analysis (what is a 'public of militants' as the 'public image of a party?') are completely obscured in Stalinist terms by the traditional vision.

It is the same obscurantism that reigns over the new philosophers and their vision of the Gulag, and Althusser could well diverge from our master dissidents – he re-uses the same regressive form of analysis: neo-humanism opposed to a retro-totalitarianism, the reactivation of an old concept of the State and its powers that is founded on a conception of political space that is still panoptic (the State of surveillance and of the Gulag). Recycling, with respect to liberty, the Right, responsibility, autonomy, dissidence ... . It is exactly Althusser's feigned offensive scenario against the party. The eternal phantom of the great manipulator Subject, the State, the apparatus, power, and the small oppressed subject, but who will become large: civil society, the militant, the dissident. Eternal polarity of Stalinism that conforms to the analysis of such a comfortable space! Eternal thought subjugated and trapped in the nostalgia of the political and a State power that has at bottom no credit except through the grief of authoritarianism that is attributed to it. The true Stalinism is that of this 'critical' thought that wants, at all costs, to believe in the Stalinism of the adversary – thus resuscitating it in the moment of its weakness.

Everything that appeals to de-Stalinization, autonomy, dissidence, and transparency, is of the same order of analytic debility. And everything happens as if French society mandated Althusser to channel all deception towards this traditional and dusty problematic: protect the CP under a Stalinism of complacency – the 'radical' critique was never anything more than an ideological reinforcement, a dialectical graft onto the body without organs of the party!

Fleeing the test of the truth of power, the CP normally finds itself facing the legitimacy of its own power. What is left of an apparatus that does not want to take power? The crucial question that is posed concerns not its strategy or its errors (another diversion), but its *raison d'être*. What sense can a party have that redirects its proper historical finality? 'It no longer serves a purpose', Rocard says pragmatically. It's worse: it is disqualified in its very existence, it runs the risk of never recuperating from this test of truth, it has never known how to respond to this challenge. And I speak here as a militant, which I am not, but whose personal despair I understand in terms not so much of political defeat as of symbolic humiliation.

Thank God for the example the party gives to its militants, the big courageous example of renouncing striving for power and remaining in a pious, propitious, and constructive opposition. The grand example will undoubtedly be followed by the militants in relation to their own apparatus: they know that serenity comes from sacrifice and they must guard themselves against all revolutionary metabolism – they could have verified that it is through involutions and defeat that the party succeeded. With respect to French society as a whole – they will not put this beautiful dissuasive architecture into question again without taking into account that the apparatus and the party are today the only things in France that offer a veritable *disciplinary reception structure* where it can situate itself, come what may, in relation to the apparatus's decisions. What extraordinary security (the army is less certain).

Even if the party line is geometrically variable, it is still a line, and in the world where everything floats, where everyone is left to his own desires, in the agony of doing and thinking what one wants at the moment where the will as referent disappears, let us admire that at least this dictatorship of the line persists, along with the security that it furnishes, and which is well worth the dictatorship of free expression that we otherwise want to impose on ourselves. The CP is the most beautiful protective and therapeutic institution in the Western world. Let's not decry it in the name of a gossipy reformism or self-critical conformism. Is it necessary, after the dictatorship of the proletariat, to renounce the dictatorship of the party? Nothing suggests that this would be an objective progress. We have known for a long time that freedom of speech and desire is the modern and globalized form of surveillance and silence. Do I dare put forth what I am saying here once again in the name of the rank and file? If I were a militant I would have nothing to do with a party that was vulnerable to modernism, vulnerable to all of the winds of history, vulnerable to my own critique. If I was not a militant, I would have nothing to do with a 'critical' party, renovated and recycled in the colours of speech and desire – I want the party to be confronted by its radical weakening and its death.

2. The State of Grace

a. September 1981. *The Ecstasy of Socialism*

> A painful idea: that beyond a certain precise point in time, history was longer real. Without realizing it the whole of the human species would have suddenly left reality. Everything that would have happened since would no longer be at all true, but we would be unaware of this. Our present task and duty would be to discover this point and, as long as we have not grasped it, we would have to persevere in the present destruction.

Canetti

My hypothesis is that we in France are currently in an ecstatic form of socialism.

It is enough to see the gloomy ecstasy on Mitterrand's face.

Ecstasy characterizes the passage to a pure state, in its pure form, a form without content and without passion. Ecstasy is antinomic to passion.

We can thus speak of an ecstasy of the State. Dispassionate, disincarnated, disaffected, but all-powerful in its transparency, the State accedes to its ecstatic form, which is that of the transpolitical. At the same time no one believes in this and there is a kind of total oblation, a total appeal, a universal solicitation toward this unique figure that, from a political point of view, has itself disappeared or is in the process of disappearing: the State.

It is the same for socialism, and its state of grace would at bottom be this: the outrageous assumption of a model that has lost its truth along the way.

The Left did not overturn the Right by means of a rupture, nor did it succeed the Right by alternation. Something strange happened with this Left's mode of arrival, which otherwise was correlative to the Right's mode of disappearance. The latter has simply been erased, like something that no longer existed. We doubted this, but the Left itself has not existed for a long time either. This did not prevent its fantastic reappearance in one fell swoop, its resuscitation, as if it were the fundamental calling of French society, as if it were an eternal heritage (which was, moreover, immediately sanctified by all sorts of commemorative ceremonies: the Panthéon, Mont Valérien, etc.). Its promotion is thus inscribed as the crowning moment of the year of national heritage.

This is properly neither a revolution nor a historical episode, but a sort of long-retarded post-historical birthing (such that one could have long believed it had been definitively aborted), a very peculiar sort of delivery, like that of a hidden child that capital had conceived behind the back of French society. It germinates, incubates, explodes and invades everything in a single stroke. It is just like *Alien*. The Left is the monster in *Alien*. And this event, taken as a whole, appears like some gigantic special effect – a quite successful one moreover – a brief ecstasy in the morose course of our popular destiny.

I would like to believe that all of this was the fruit of a long social and political struggle on the part of workers, unions, leftist parties, and countless individual wills and initiative – but I am not quite certain that this is the case.

Nor do I believe that people had any illusion about the political substance of the elections, but they did make use of it in their own way – cinematographically, so to speak: they drew from the electoral medium a special effect, a wager on the Left which suddenly had all the luck. 'We won!' But take note, this spectacular confidence is in the form of a challenge: one treats oneself to the Left. The representatives of the people are quite naïve: they take their election as approval, a popular consensus; they still never suspect that there is nothing more ambiguous than putting someone in power, that the most enjoyable spectacle for the people has undoubtedly always been the political class's failure.

Somewhere in the depths of the celebrated *popular consciousness* the political class, whoever composes it, remains the fundamental enemy. At least we have to hope so.

Nor do I believe that this electoral *acting out* involves a well-defined projection of the hopes of the majority, an allegiance to socialism as a will to representation. Rather, I think the aesthetic and moral indignation has been touched, but as for the rest, for the historical and political imagination, this event is inconsequential. It is the ecstasy that counts. Things are changing; they are going to change! We don't believe in a finality or historical surpassing, but bring a vague impulse to consent, a vague desire to believe that we grant the effects of innovation, the effects of change, indeed, the effects of fashion. And I don't say this lightly or metaphorically. With this politically asexual socialism, with this ecstatic and asexual socialism, I think that we are literally entering into the era of the ready-to-believe (*prêt-à-croire*), just as fashion has entered the era of ready-to-wear (fashion is also ecstatic and transsexual).

The advent of socialism as a *model* is altogether different from its emergence. As an event, a myth, a force of rupture, socialism does not have, how shall we put it, the time to resemble itself, to acquire the force of a model, it does not have the time to merge with society – in this respect it is not a stable State, and moreover has only made brief historical appearances. Today, however, it presents itself as a stable and credible model – and yet it is no longer a revolutionary exigency, but a simulation of change (simulation in the sense of the development of the best possible scenario) and a simulation of the future. No surprises, no violence, no excess, no real passion. Like all models, this one will be realized as its own complete look-alike; it is made to hyper-realize itself. This is why I say that it is ecstatic: the hyper-real is the ecstasy of the real congealed within its own resemblance, relieved of its imaginary and frozen in its model (even if this model is that of change).

All of this is raised in order to pose the question upon which depend the full stakes of the situation and the very possibility of understanding anything about it. Does this socialism imply a resurrection of politics and the political scene? Does it imply a deceleration of the transpolitical process whereby time and history are fading – whereby change becomes a generalized process of the dissuasion of political and social stakes, a process of the disappearance of the real and the trans-appearance of all models – the State as the ecstatic model of society's fulfilment, terror as the ecstatic model of violence's fulfilment, etc.?

I am not going to respond. This precisely is the blindspot Canetti is speaking about wherein, without realizing it, the entire human species would have taken leave of reality. This is our fundamental concern: the reality or unreality of the situation. Everything gets played out here and, unfortunately, it seems that our concern lies outside of the purview of critical thought. This is the crucial dilemma. Barring some miraculous reversion of the situation that delivers it body and soul to some social project, that is, to reality, we must, as Canetti says, persevere in the present destruction.

The assumption of the critical values of theory in socialism is a part of the ecstasy. Ecstatic, they henceforth look down at us ironically from the height of power.

But theoretical concepts never offer a real alternative – and there must be no mistake about this. In their most radical exercise they cause reality to wobble; they are a challenge to the real. And they must remain so, under pain of turning against you in the form of a value judgement, in the form of a principle, and in particular of that reality principle in which they are supposed to knock a hole.

The metaphor must remain a metaphor, the concept a concept. Too bad for the intellectuals.

Of late, however, this is what is happening: with the assumption of the socialist alternative under the sign of political power, the materialization of the entire conceptual system of values (progress, the morals of history, the rationality of politics, the creative imagination, and, *last but not least*, the transfiguration of virtue by the philosopher-king – in short, the entire Platonic ideal that is at base that of the intellectual class, even if the latter denounces it).

'68 was not a mistake – '68 did not put the imagination in power, it was content with its joyous assumption in the imaginary, and its joyous suicide, which, historically speaking, is the most courteous form of success. '68 exalted the social's poetic exigency, the inversion of reality and desire, and not their virtuous reconciliation in the enactment of socialism. '68 has happily remained a violent metaphor, without ever becoming a reality. Today the imaginary has descended from the unreal walls of Nanterre into the ministerial drawers. And this surreptitiously circumvents the whole position of the intellectual.

How can one function in the accession of the promise, the idea's pretension to reality, in the shift from speech to the right to speech, in the legislation of all the illegal metaphors, in the realist illusion of the social? Even from a political perspective, one is confronted with a sort of fundamental error. For this will to reconcile the course of society with a voluntary and coherent project, this will to realize the ever-fallacious promise of the political (which, as Machiavelli noted, is truly effective only when fallacious), this will is deadly, and deathly tedious. It is what within socialism is contrary to all sense.

But this is another story. In any case today power is left to people (and this applies not only to socialists) who have explicitly renounced its exercise, who have nothing political left and openly declare themselves incapable of dealing with ambiguity, or dealing in the immorality of discourse which is the very mechanism of worldly ambition (as both Machiavelli and the Jesuits would agree) and are faithful to the transparency of the idea. What, then, is left for intellectuals, for whom the transparency of the idea is a profession of faith? If the social begins to operate on the basis of good will, then what remains, to be truly political, than to operate with ill will?

> It is the State that holds vigil on the dream. It is reality that incarnates it.
>
> F. Régis Bastide

The new power considers itself cultural and intellectual. It no longer wants to be a cynical historical force, but wants to be the incarnation of values. Having betrayed its political essence, it wants intellectuals, on their part, to betray theirs, and become reconciled to the concept. It wants intellectuals to lose their sense of the duplicity of the concept, as they have lost their sense of the duplicity of politics, so they can move to the side of the real and the imaginary. This is the contract being proposed by this power that is not one – democracy at its peak, the hypocritical power of virtue – and we are caught in the trap. For the intellectual, unfortunately, is always sufficiently virginal to be complicit in the repression of vice. S/he is not up to the cynical – i.e. immoral and ambiguous – exercise of thought, no more than politicians are up to the cynical exercise of power.

In reality, we do not have to be too afraid because this kind of socialism is no more than the simulacrum of an alternative – it is not exactly an event, but the posthumous materialization of a bygone ideology. It is the form taken by a model, and not by a myth, nor even by history. Having no illusion about its own foundational force, it proposes itself as simply credible and having illusions about its underlying political passions; it appears as pathos, a moral and historical artefact. Against the pious simulacrum of socialism, which has finally ended up, after so many failures on the shores of power, against this ethical phantom we can do nothing, just as the thought of the revolution, which was powerful against capital, lies prostrate before the phantom of capital.

The simulated order robs us of all power of denial; simulated socialism robs us of all power of participation. We have analysed the values it simulates (progress, profit, and production – Enlightenment, history, and rationality) and reduced their claim to *reality*, but we have not abolished them as simulacra, as second-hand spectres: being transparent and insubstantial, these cannot be assailed. And it is this second-hand socialist spectre that today haunts Europe. We wander amongst the phantoms of capital: from now on we wander through the posthumous model of socialism. All this hyper-reality is not going to change one iota; in a sense it has long been our familiar surrounding. We are sick with a political leukaemia, and this growing indifference (we are traversed by power without being affected, and we traverse power without affecting it) is altogether similar to the most modern kind of pathology: that is, not objective biological aggression, but the organism's growing incapacity to produce antibodies (or even, as in multiple sclerosis, the possibility of the antibodies turning against the body itself).

Thus, socialism in power is only a later phase in the pretentious disenchantment of this society. However, something here catches us a little off-guard. For it is the first time that the collective cultural pathos, that the remnants of political and moral utopia, scattered among the debris of a society swept clean by the salubrious ideological catastrophe of '68, is thus promoted on the stage in order to be operationalized as a phantom. In the past twenty years we have experienced the promotion of the economy as a gigantic referential prosthesis, as the surface support of every collective impulse, unassailable in its presumed objectivity. Not only are judgements of fact derived from this, but so are judgements of value and political decisions. (Certainly everything plays on the simulation of political rationality, about which no one understands anything anymore, but what does it matter? The fiction of the economy's jurisdiction can become all-powerful – it became the true collective convention.) Now another collective convention is being put forward: morality and culture are being materialized as prostheses of government. Social prothesis and culture prothesis ('your ideas interest us', 'your desires interest us', 'your creativity interests us' – the banker at the BNP [Banque national de Paris] was more frank: 'your money interests us', and the people of the Third World more brutal: 'your garbage interests us') and the reinvention, after too much objective management drove people to indifference, of a social subjectivity, of a social affectivity resting on its dead (Panthéon), digging in the ruins of the historical imaginary for the material with which to synthesize a puppet of the collective will.

And we the intellectuals find ourselves trapped. For as long as it was a matter of the economy, of the programming and disenchantment of a liberal society, we retained inner integrity, well provided with indefinite mental and political resources, the vestals of a small critical and philosophical flame, with the promise of theory's silent efficacity (and theory, moreover, was doing quite well; it will no doubt never again recover the offensive and jubilant quality, along with the imposing sinecure, which it enjoyed these past twenty years).

The vital forces were just where they were, that is to say, elsewhere, in another France, well short of power, in the shadows of tomorrow. How aberrant and how perilous to propel these living forces in the direction of business! Nothing could be worse than having the force of theory absorbed within an institution. The very utopia of concepts with which we analysed this situation that was not our own and that we dissolved into its imaginary components, this very utopia turns against us in the form of real value judgements, of an intellectual jurisdiction, armed with our own weapons, in the form of this phantom of a collective will, be it that of our own class, which retains, even in simulation, the power to annul us. As guardians of the sublime distortion of signs and the real, we are trapped, paralysed by the staging of their reconciliation.

It is like a chemical precipitation that solidifies crystals and puts an end to the solution in suspension through a resolution whose effect is irreversible.

We have no more enemies. The best (subjectively speaking), because they are in power, are also the worst (objectively speaking). Pragmatically speaking, because all pragmatics are paradoxical, we cannot escape it – we are also in a sort of double bind, an insoluble dilemma (and not a historical contradiction): we are called on to really participate in an unreal, second-hand event as if it were real and first-hand. Rare are those events that occur at their proper time: some are premature, others arrive after the fact and are naught but the recycling of a failed turn of history. *Simulatio post-mortem*. There are miscarriages after term just like there are miscarriages before term. This is one of them. The coming of socialism not through enthusiasm but through disaffection, not by historical rupture but by historical exhaustion (as relayed by the retroactive state of the average French citizen), this coming by default of a historical model that lost its truth on the way belongs very much to the realm of recycling and simulation, but it demands that we act *as* if it was the original. (This does not mean that the actors of this socialist psychodrama are liars or dupes – their integrity or enthusiasm [at least that of some of them] is not in question. Unfortunately, it's more serious: what is in question is the integrity and originality of the historical event itself.) We are thus called on to simulate in return, to act as if we were being led by the irresistible progress of history, and as if all of this coincided with, by some strange formal resemblance, the hope for a life change. (An old slogan of Rimbaud, now taken up by socialism – enjoy yourselves, today we will really change life – it's marvellous! The metaphor always collapses into reality.)

This dilemma in which we are left is not all. There is something else to denounce, even if it is quite difficult to do so, and which bears on the profound confusion of every socialist project, even if its intentions are pure – they are no less naïve. I return to Mandeville and his *Fable of the Bees* where he shows (in the eighteenth century, some will say, but the French Revolution changed all that – still, I don't believe it) that it's not a society's morality, nor its positive system of values, that causes it to change and progress, but its immorality and its vices, its misalignment relative to its own proper values. This is in a way the secret of politics: this structural duplicity in the functioning of societies, which is something very different from the psychological duplicity of those in power. A duplicity that, in some deep sense, turns the social process into a *game*, whereby society eludes its own sociability, and survives thanks to the flexibility of appearances, to this detachment, this immoral strategy (which is no doubt collective, but neither visible nor concerted, which is instead, for society, disconcerting) relative to its own values.

This is completely opposed (and this is why I say that they have lost all sense of politics) to the belief of socialists and of all sociologists as well – that every society is, to all intents and purposes, social, that is to say, in alignment with its own values and consistent in its collective project. The problem, then, is to reconcile society with its own project and to 'socialize' that which in truth wants to be socialized. The annihilation of all duplicity, of every strategy of appearance at the level of values – the maximization of the social bond, the intensification of collective responsibility (and, to be sure, of control), the visibility of the social structures and their functioning, the apotheosis of public morality and culture: this is the socialist dream, mad with transparency, dripping with naïveté. What group ever functioned in this manner and, more importantly, what group ever dreamed of doing so? It is happily apparent that no social project worthy of its name ever existed, that no group at bottom *ever ideally conceived of itself as social*, in short, that there has never existed *even* the shadow (except in the heads of intellectuals) nor the embryo of a collective subject with limited liability, nor even the possibility of an objective of this kind. Societies that so devote their energies, who set out on this moral dream of socialization, are lost from the outset. It is the most basic nonsense. Fortunately, these societies escape from themselves; the social will not have taken place.

Translated by Mark Lajoie

Notes

Excerpt from *La Gauche Divine*, Paris: Bernard Grasset, 1985, pp. 13–83.

1. Insofar as they are revolutionaries, things are certainly very different, and there will be much to say about this. Because, between capital's immorality, which is the resource of the exercise of power, and the incurable morality that henceforth prohibits communists from political exercise (the two historically associating together), another path had been beaten by the proletariat of the nineteenth century, a frontal challenge to power by death, in crushed insurrections, and singularly in the Commune. Marx had been reproached for not taking an interest in workers' struggles until after they were defeated (*Class Struggles in France, Eighteenth Brumaire, The Commune*). No fool this Marx. Because it is at this point that they become interesting: when the historical subject is crushed. Because it is then that Marx is immoral and foresees something in the destruction of what is most valuable to him: this linear finality of the dialectic of Reason, this victorious proletarian reason – does he perhaps know in depth the absurdity of all this and of attempts to take power? Perhaps had he pondered longer on power, sniffed out Lenin and Stalin and, behind this ascending calculus of history, reckoned that the crushing of 'the class' (insensate breakdown of the class-subject, there, all of a sudden, and without waiting for the reasonable breakdown of the dominant class) was still the only possible challenge. At bottom, the only good proletariat, like a good Indian, is a dead one. But this is true in another sense, one fatal for all power or bureaucracy. At certain moments in history the proletariat played a part in its own destruction (*contra* Marx himself, cf. the Commune), and in exchange for no present or future power, but against all power. This doesn't fit into any dialectic, forever unnamed, but some part of this death energy shows through today in the derision of all institutions, including the revolutionary ones, that had thought to bury it.

2. *Trans. note*. Luciano Lama was the head of the General Confederation of Italian Labour, the Communist-dominated union sometimes called the farmer's union because of its post-war roots in southern agriculture.

3. *Trans. note*. See the articles by Althusser published in *Le Monde* on the 25, 26, 27 and 29 April 1978. The diatribes against Marchais actually began earlier, on 6 April. But the attack on the CP's lack of democratic process and the bourgeois military structure of the party itself spilled over from the 25th to the 27th during the period of its 23rd Congress. Althusser does appear to commit himself to the view, of which Baudrillard makes so much, that the CP is not a party of government. Althusser continued to speak out in interviews during May, and he became so unpopular with party militants that stalls selling his books at the young Communists' Fête d'Avant-Garde were overturned. For a blow-by-blow account see R.W. Johnson, *The Long March of the French Left* (London: Macmillan, 1981), pp. 231ff. Althusser's pieces were translated into English and published by the *New Left Review* in May–June 1978.

Dropping Out of History

Interview with Sylvère Lotringer

Sylvère Lotringer: At a time when the French Socialists are finally back in power, it may sound inappropriate or unfair to talk about the end of history, or the end of politics. Are the French Socialists too exhausted or their hands too tied-up to measure up to the event? But what is an event in a history that is dropping out of sight? However paradoxical it may sound, especially with regards to Jean Baudrillard, a case could be made that everything of importance in French culture has originated much less from Marx and Freud, those great founding fathers, than from a kind of orphan of an event – obsessive and enigmatic: May '68. At last in the land of structure and of political centralism, the event precedes the reflection upon it. Since then it has spawned much thought, of course, even if this reflection upon the event sometimes seems to turn its back on all that this revolution – which wasn't one – was supposed to have represented: spontaneity, anarchy, revolutionary romanticism.

May '68 took everybody by surprise. It swept down on France like an avalanche, and it disappeared almost immediately, mysteriously, practically without leaving any traces behind, consuming all the answers. But it has invented a new question. It is to this question that Baudrillard, like some other French thinkers (with whom he is not always in agreement), explored to the point of putting into doubt all the certainties upon which we relied: our social system, the possibility of political action, our sense of history and even the very reality of our society.

How can an event escape the logic of politics?

Jean Baudrillard: Politics has functioned classically in terms of distinguishable contrasts: the Left or the Right, as elsewhere the true or the false, the beautiful or the ugly, etc. Now at a given moment the energy of a situation has ceased to depend on this kind of dissociation. It is no longer the dialectic of the two terms which organizes things, but the fact that the forms go their own way – but crazily. It is this which I call the 'ecstasy of forms', their own self-enchantment: this is the truer than true, the falser than false. A form runs amok in a kind of logic which precludes all reserve, retreat or recollection, like cancer cells shooting forth on their own organic course. This logic seems more interesting to me because it corresponds more to the evolution of things today.

SL: And where do you see this logic currently at work?

JB: In the world of fashion, which illustrates this phenomenon perfectly. Fashion depends on no aesthetic judgement. It's not the beautiful opposed to the ugly, it's what is more beautiful than the beautiful. The obese, that famous fat American, is not opposed to the skinny one. He is fatter than fat, and that is what is fascinating. Fashion is the ecstatic form of the beautiful, its absolute formalization. It functions by means of unconditional transmutation of forms. Ecstatic forms can be very static and cold; sometimes they can be warmer, more enchanting. Fashion can exclude this kind of 'hot' ecstasy. There is a splendour of fashion, beneath which we can see at work an uncontrollable, objective cult of the game. A rule which conveys the objective irony of fashion.

SL: Can fashion serve as a model for politics?

JB: Fashion has always been at odds with politics. The way it operates cannot be negated by any system of this kind. You can't oppose fashion politically to politics. It is a ritual which cannot be programmed.

SL: Must all political rituals necessarily be programmed?

JB: Unpredictable forms – forms that resist formulation and judgement – are of course much more fascinating, and therefore terribly dangerous for the powers that be, because they are no longer possible to control. These are what I call seductive forms. At a given moment a category or a form can no longer be articulated – that is, described or represented. It can no longer enter upon the scene of representation: it turns back upon itself and, taking that turn, its speed is vastly accelerated. Suddenly you have gone into a situation of weightlessness. Fascism was something like this, which is why it has remained inexplicable in political terms – as caused by the class struggle, capitalism, etc.

SL: Does May '68 partake, in its way, in this kind of snowballing of forms?

JB: There is something in May '68 which escapes our historicity. I'm not saying that it came from another planet: it is a strangeness coming out of the logic our own system generates, but not from its history.

SL: You often evoke the end of history, once in a while you also throw around provocative formulae: the end of production, of the social, of politics. Have we really reached the point where all these stakes have ceased to count? Has the time now come to consign to the wax museum everything that made up our reality? I've often felt myself that it's difficult to finish with anything. What allows you in the final analysis to say such things?

JB: I don't know if it's really an end. The word is probably meaningless in any case. For there to be an end, you would have to have linearity, and we're no longer so sure that there's such a thing. I would prefer to begin, even if it seems a little like science fiction, with a quotation from a recent work of Elias Canetti.[1] It is possible, he said, and the thought is painful for him, that starting from a precise moment in time the human race has dropped out of history, that without even being conscious of the change, humanity suddenly left reality behind; in fact, we wouldn't have been able to be conscious of this event. What we have to do now, continues Canetti, would be to find that critical point, that spot in time that we have been blind to: otherwise we just continue on with our self-destructive ways.

This hypothesis seems appealing to me because Canetti talks not about an end but about a passage, or rather what I would call an 'ecstasy' in its primal meaning: a passage at the same time into the dissolution and transcendence of a form.

SL: Did May '68 succeed in transcending politics?

JB: It is a prodigious effect, a kind of pure object or event, the first event that I can think of that is situated on the other side of that crucial point Canetti is talking about. Past this point, you can no longer manipulate effects through causes.

SL: You can always manipulate causes among themselves. Nietzsche was well aware of this (and had to pay the costs of his insight) – that the cause of an event is always imagined after the fact. The cause is added to the event in order to regulate it, or regularize it – to keep it within bounds.

After that joyful May, we were treated to the curious spectacle of causes racing after effects that had become ever more elusive. But no explanation has succeeded in diminishing one iota the pure surprise of the event.

JB: That pure event which comes like a fatality without explanation or referent. From now on you can no longer attribute things to clear causes. The event is an object which derives its overwhelming necessity precisely from its being isolated and disconnected, as is the case with a catastrophe. This is a necessity well beyond any rational finality. This kind of event, of word or being, which absorbs all attempts at explanation, which comes across as pure evidence, alien to any causal or final order, or which is more final than the final, that *is* fatal. May '68 is a fatal event. It is an event that we have been unable to rationalize and exploit – and from which we have been able to conclude nothing.

SL: It outraced everybody.

JB: When the effect goes faster than the cause, it devours it. I could easily see the 'speed-up' analysed by Paul Virilio from this angle, as an attempt to accelerate faster than linearity can handle. Speed is different from movement. Movement goes somewhere, speed nowhere.

SL: May '68 is an event that had no consequences.

JB: There is a certain power in the fact of being inconsequential. Behind the political, revolutionary, historical scene and also failure, there is the power of an event which manages to absorb its own continuity and makes it implode, which succeeds in swallowing its own energy and disappearing. We witness the annihilation of causes. Those kind of things are exciting.

SL: May '68 is an event without cause. As soon as the effect leaps the chain of causes, the event takes off. It outraces any effort to understand or to master it. At this point, its trajectory becomes properly *incalculable*.

JB: May '68 has remained indecipherable. It has been the forerunner of nothing. You might wonder then what remains when one has tried everything in an effort to explain it. Perhaps a kind of 'secret' is involved here. There are fundamentally two kinds of secrets. The obscene form of secret involves a saturation of the event with explanations. The other kind of secret involves something which is not hidden, and therefore cannot be expressed directly in words. It is this second kind of secret which makes the event somehow innocent.

SL: There is also a secret of Fascism?

JB: Yes. The secret lies in this total autonomy of a story, a form, an event that can no longer be described in a logical, coherent and acceptable manner, but which runs totally wild. Past a certain threshold of inertia, the forms start snowballing, terror is unleashed as an empty form. The effect of being swept away feeds on itself and, like Fascism, can become the source of immense energies.

SL: Fascism is, above all, an effect of panic. So it needed at once a scapegoat in order to exorcize the fear of the abyss.

JB: Panic is the catastrophic form of ecstasy. I say 'catastrophic' in the almost neutral meaning of the word, in its mathematical sense. It is one of the effects of ecstasy, of the strange response of the object-world to the subject-world, of an utterly external destiny which comes as absolute surprise and whose symbolic wave collides with the human world. So what do you do with this kind of event? Do you allow your life to be changed? Ordinarily when something like this, something surprising, occurs, you try to comprehend it as a subject, to fit it into your own subjective patterns. But here you have had to renounce precisely this quality to channel all your subjective energy back onto the object.

SL: The event becomes a reflecting object, an imaginary mirror sending each one back to his own fantasy without ever letting itself be touched. There are no children of May.

JB: The event has been eclipsed without leaving a trace, except this secondary effect of parody, this second- or third-hand product made to occupy a political scene that has been utterly absorbed and destroyed: socialism.

SL: French socialism has done everything to present itself as the heir of '68. But it is a cause without energy or vitality. It barely succeeds in being the parody of its own history.

JB: What is intolerable about May '68, its hard, indestructible kernel, is the event's sheer gratuity. It was produced like a destiny, beyond the point of political vacuum that socialism inhabits now with a commemorative ceremony at the Panthéon, a military parade on 14 July and all these thundering social measures that come fifty years too late.

SL: The ecstasy of socialism is a simulation that is ashamed of itself, a world without surprise or secret. History at last suited to itself.

JB: Yes. Nothing to do with the happy hyper-simulation of fashion. It's the cold side of ecstasy. Its ecstasy is to be truer than true. It creates a kind of dizziness, an effect of escalated truth. As a model, it's pretty sad and tawdry. Socialism realizes, hyper-realizes, a model which no longer has any veracity, or any original passion.

SL: The socialists are setting up a stage-décor in *trompe-l'oeil* to hide the fact that socialism has disappeared. Like history, it has no real substance, nor any particular meaning. It is no more than a shadow of itself. It is no longer seductive. It is no longer anything to worry about.

JB: History is now in state of simulation, like a body that is kept in a state of hibernation. This is a kind of irreversible coma where things continue nevertheless to function, and eventually can even seem to amount to history; and then surreptitiously, as Canetti has it, it is possible that everything which has happened since that point in time would no longer be true. In any case, we would no longer be in a position to decide on its truth or falsity.

SL: The end you talk about, then, that would be rather the end of all finality – together with its exacerbated, empty parody of a resurgence.

JB: I would prefer not to play the role of the lugubrious, thoroughly useless prophet. There is no end in the sense that God is dead, or that history is dead. It is not a tragic end, one that would be highly charged with emotion, an end that you could mourn – for in that case there would be at least something to be done about it. Things have just been progressing in a certain direction, then suddenly there is a curve in the road, a turning point. Somewhere in the historical, political, even psychological, scene, the *real* scene, where you had rules for the game and some solid stakes that everybody could believe in, has been lost.

SL: Why was it lost?

JB: I'm not about to be explaining things. That's fiction. History has stopped meaning, referring to anything – whether you call it social space or the real. We have passed into a kind of hyper-reality where things are being replaced *ad infinitum*.

SL: Societies with no history have mythology; we, on the other hand, have turned mythology into history. If we now are able to cease believing in this history, if we can put its very reality into doubt, it may be because history has had a lot to do with faith.

JB: But what then does it mean to believe? To believe would be, all the same, to maintain a kind of subjectivity that would guarantee the solidity of things and serve as a criterion for meaning. If sense is dependent on belief, then we remain trapped irremediably in the realm of the imaginary. What interests me instead, but I'm not so sure you can still call it history, is the possibility of a pure event, an event that is no longer tied to the existence of a subject and hence is no longer available for manipulation, interpretation or deciphering by any historical subjectivity.

SL: Can the subject then be totally short-circuited by the event?

JB: The problematic of the subject involves the postulation that reality can be *represented*, that things give off signs which guarantee their existence and significance – in short, that there is a principle of reality. All of that is now collapsing with the dissolution of the subject. This is of course the well-known 'crisis of representation'. But just because this system of values is coming apart, which also supported the political and theatrical scenes, doesn't mean that we have been left in a complete vacuum. My position is by no means a nihilist one. If you explore the terrain of value in order to root out its last vestiges, you are left, on the contrary, in a situation that is even more radical. The radicality is to arrive at isolating, in things, all that makes for interpretation, all that weighs them down with sense, all that overdetermines them with meaning.

SL: So, then, what is left, once you have gotten rid of this burden of sense?

JB: Much less than we would have thought. All the traditional systems of value in terms of energy, for example, now seem to teeter on the brink.

SL: Your analysis recalls, though, in many ways that proposed by Gilles Deleuze and Félix Guattari in *Anti-Oedipus*: leaving representation behind, rejection of the dialectic, critique of meaning, etc. You part with them on the terrain of subjectivity: they fragment the subject, you abolish it; they make of desire the basis of becoming, you see becoming as involving the annihilation of desire.

JB: I couldn't care less about desire. I wouldn't know any longer where to put it. I neither want to abolish it nor to take it into account. What bothers me about desire is the idea of a force or energy which would be the common source of all these fluxes. Is desire really involved? In my opinion, desire has nothing to do with it.

SL: Well, then, what has?

JB: Things just don't happen anymore dialectically. These are no longer situations where a subject is involved: they happen all by themselves, without any mediation, by a sort of instantaneous commutation.

SL: Do these events respond to any objective criteria? What strategy could we adopt that would take into account these situations where the subject no longer has a valid place?

JB: A strategy of the object. A kind of objective irony. Do you know the story of Beau Brummell? He travelled a lot, always accompanied by his servant. One day he arrived in Scotland. There were many lochs, one more beautiful than the other. Brummell turned to his servant and asked him: 'Which loch do I prefer?' Having to choose is really a bore. That's what servants are for. That's not what counts in any case. Power – Knowledge – Will, let those who invented these ideas take responsibility for them. It makes perfect sense to me that the great masses, very snobbishly, delegate to the class of intellectuals, of politicians, this business of managing, of choosing, of knowing what one wants. They're joyously getting rid of those burdensome categories which no one, deep down inside, really wants any part of. That people want to be told what they want is certainly not true, that they really want knowledge is not evident either, and that they desire to want it is also by no means clear. The entire edifice of socialism is based on that assumption.

SL: The objective irony would be the careless manner in which the masses get rid of their responsibilities, turning power back to its fantasies, knowledge to its obsessions, will to its illusions. The silent majority, as you see it then, is not the accomplice of law and order. Its silence is rather a silence of death. The masses play dead; and this stubborn silence, this insolent reserve, would sanction the end – excuse me, the disappearance – of the social.

JB: Exactly. No one wants to bother about these problems. The great systems of information relieve the masses of the care of having to know, understand, be informed, to be up on things. Advertising relieves people of the care of having to choose, which is perfectly human and understandably a torment. As to power, it has always seemed ironic to me to delegate it to someone: this is like catching it in a trap, and this trap closes on the political class itself. I see all of this as a profound reversal of strategy on the part of the masses: they are no longer involved in a process of subversion or of revolution, but in some gigantic devolution from an unwanted liberty – with some evil genie behind all of this.

SL: Insofar as we can conceive of a reversal of strategy, the political stakes are not entirely a dead letter.

JB: I see no strategy being possible, except that of an object which no one could claim.

SL: Do you see an object-strategy in the rising to extremes projected by Virilio – the military class devouring civil society before disappearing in its turn on its suicidal course?

JB: The calculation of Paul is to push the military to a kind of extreme absolute of power that can ultimately only cause its own downfall, place it before the judgement of a God and absorb it into the society it destroys. He carries out this calculation with such an identification or obsession that I can credit him only with a powerful sense of irony: the system devours its own principle of reality, outbids on its own vacuous form until it attains to an absolute end or limit, to its ironical destiny of reversal. I myself am not so interested in military 'hardware'; in the 'software', rather. It's rather in its form that his idea seems valid to me. I think the strategy of irony is to let the system collapse on the thrust of its own energy. Not being able to fight it directly, all you can do is rely on a logic of provocation.

SL: Dare the system to destroy itself! Politics in that case could only survive in its own disappearance.

JB: What I think will occur is a transmutation of all forms and the consequent unfeasibility of all politics. In fact, I don't even see on the political level what would be equivalent to forms runnning wild, except that we would probably have to construct another theory of the media as *agents provocateurs* of an oversupply of information, of an annihilating ecstasy making of the substance of traditional political debate a gigantic abyss.

SL: Wouldn't the critique of media be, in the final analysis, the ghost they carry with them, an echo of complicity which the media must utter in order to justify their existence? For there to be mystification there has to be somewhere a standard of truth.

JB: There remains behind all of this a certain symbolic claim to truth. The media are denounced as a fabulous distortion, but where does the distortion come from? If you put the media into the system will–choice–liberty, you can't do anything more with them. You can only say they push the political subject back into total alienation, say that it is power which manipulates, etc. Let's eliminate the idea that the media mystify and alienate. Enough is enough.

Notes

Originally published in *Impulse* [Toronto] (Spring/Summer 1983): 10–13.

1. *Editor's Note.* Baudrillard often refers to this quote from *Canetti's The Human Province* (New York: Seabury, 1978). See above in 'The Divine Left'.

Our Theatre of Cruelty

Mogadishu

In the terrorist act there is a simultaneous power of death and simulation which it is intolerable to see confused with the 'morbid taste of death', and with the frenzy of the 'morbid' and the 'spectacular'. Dead or living, it is elsewhere that terrorism wins out. At least by this single fact: it alone makes the event, and thus returns the whole 'political' order to its nullity. And the media, all the while orchestrating the victory of order, only cause the evidence for the opposite to reverberate: to wit, that terrorism is burying the political order.

The media are terrorists in their own fashion, working continually to produce (good) sense, but, at the same time, violently defeating it by arousing everywhere a fascination without scruples, that is to say, a paralysis of meaning, to the profit of a single scenario.

Terrorism is not violent in itself; only the spectacle it unleashes is truly violent. It is our Theatre of Cruelty, the only one that remains to us, perhaps equal in every respect to that of Artaud or to that of the Renaissance, and extraordinary in that it brings together *the spectacular and the challenge at their highest points*. It is at the same time a model of simulation, a micro-model flashing with a minimally real event and a maximal echo chamber, like a crystal thrown into an unstable solution or an experimental matrix, an insoluble equation which makes all the variables appear suddenly. Not a real event, but a condensed narrative, a flash, a scenario – that is to say, that which opposes to every event said to be real the purest form of the spectacular – and a ritual, or that which, of all possible events, opposes to the political and historical model or order the purest symbolic form of challenge.

A strange mixture of the symbolic and the spectacular, of challenge and simulation. This paradoxical configuration is the only original form of our time, and subversive because insoluble. There is neither victory nor defeat: no sense can be made of an event which is irremediably spectacular, or irremediably symbolic. Everything in terrorism is ambivalent and reversible: death, the media, violence, victory. Who plays into the other's hands? Death itself is undefinable: the death of the terrorists is equivalent to that of the hostages; they are substitutable. In spite of all the efforts to set them into radical opposition, fascination allows no distinction to be made, and rightly so, for power finally does not make any either, but settles its accounts with everyone, and buries Baader and Schleyer together at Stuttgart in its incapacity to unravel the deaths and rediscover the fine dividing line, the distinctive and valid oppositions which are the secret of law and order. Nor is it possible to reclaim a positive use for the media, or a transparency of repression: the repressive act traverses the same unforeseeable spiral as the terrorist act; no one knows where it will stop, nor all the setbacks and reversals that will ensue. There is no distinction possible between the spectacular and symbolic, no distinction possible between the 'crime' and the 'repression'. *It is this uncontrollable eruption of reversibility that is the true victory of terrorism.*

This victory lies not at all in the fact of imposing a negotiation and forcing a government to capitulate. Besides, the objective – most of the time to liberate imprisoned comrades – is typically a zero-sum equation. The stakes are elsewhere. And if power wins out at the level of the objective, it loses at the level of real stakes. It loses its political definition, and is forced to accept, all the while trying to thwart, this reversibility of all the actors in the same process. Terrorists, killers, hostages, leaders, spectators, public opinion – there is no more innocence in a system which has no meaning. No tragedy either (in spite of the ideology of the Baader group itself, and the pedagogy of the terrorist model on a worldwide scale). The force of the terrorists comes to them precisely from the fact that they have no logic. The others do: it is quick, effective, flawless, without scruples; it is why they 'win'. If the terrorists had one, they would no longer be terrorists. To demand that they be at the same time illogical, which gives them their power, and logical tacticians, which would make them successful, is absurd – again a fantasy of synthesis, and of defence on our part, which allows us to recuperate ourselves in the fury of defeat.

Hence the stupidity and the obscenity of all that is reported about the terrorists: everywhere the wish to palm off meaning on them, to exterminate them with meaning, which is more effective than bullets of specialized commandos (and all the while subjecting them elsewhere, in the prisons, to sensory deprivation). It is still this rage for meaning which makes us, with the best will in the world, treat them like idiots incapable of going all the way and blowing up the aeroplane and the passengers, which makes us want them not to have 'won'.

Not only have they not won, but they have encouraged inordinately the sacred union of all the world forces of repression; they have reinforced the political order, etc. – let's go all the way – they have killed their Stammheim comrades, since if they had not launched and then botched this operation, the others would still be alive. But all this participates in the same conspiracy of meaning, which amounts to setting an action in contradiction with itself (here to ends that were not desired, or according to a logic which was not its own). Strangulation.

Stammheim

The insoluble polemic on the manner in which Baader and his comrades died is itself obscene, and for the same reason: there is an equal obscenity in wanting to forcibly impose meaning on the hijackers' act and in wanting to restore Baader's death to the order of factual reality. Principle of meaning as principle of truth: there you have the real lifeblood of State terrorism.

It is to believe that the German government's strategy attains perfection in a single blow: not only does it link together in an almost improvised manner the bungled taking of hostages with the immediately subsequent liquidation of the prisoners who disturbed it, but does so in such a way (coarse, equivocal, incoherent) that it traps everyone in the hysterical search for truth, which is the best way to abolish the symbolic futility of this death.

The hijackers made so many errors at Mogadishu that one can only think that they were done 'on purpose'. They have finally attained their objective obliquely, which was the challenge of their own death, the latter summing up the virtual one of all the hostages, and more radically, still, that of the power which kills them. For it absolutely must be repeated that the stakes are not to beat power on its own ground, but to oppose another political order of force. One knows nothing about terrorism if one does not see that it is not a question of real violence, nor of opposing one violence to another (which, owing to their disproportion, is absurd, and besides, all *real* violence, like real order in general, is always on the side of power), but to oppose to the *full* violence and to the *full* order a clearly superior model of extermination and virulence operating through emptiness.

The secret is to oppose to the order of the real an absolutely imaginary realm, absolutely ineffectual at the level of reality, but whose implosive energy absorbs everything real and all the violence of real power which founders there. Such a model is no longer of the order of transgression: repression and transgression are of the old order of the law, that is to say, of the order of a real *system* in expansion. In such a system, all that comes into contradiction with it, including the violence of its opposite, only makes the expansion accelerate. Here, the virulence comes from the implosion – and the death of the terrorists (or of the hostages) is of this implosive order: the abolition of value, of meaning, of the real, at a determined point. This point can be infinitesimal, and yet provokes a suction, an absorption, a gigantic convection, as could be seen at Mogadishu. Around this tiny point, the whole system of the real condenses, is tetanized, and launches all its anti-bodies. It becomes so dense that it goes beyond its own laws of equilibrium and involutes in its own over-effectiveness. At bottom, the profound tactic of simulation (for it's very much a matter of simulation in the terrorist model, and not of real death) is to provoke an excess of reality, and *to make the system collapse under it*.

If it is possible, then, to think that the hijackers have acted purposefully in order to meet their death, this kind of paradoxical death which shines intensely for a moment before falling back into the real, it is possible to think inversely that the German government itself did not commit so many errors in the Baader affair except towards a well-defined end (even without desiring it). It was able to stage Baader's death neatly – he did not do it. Far from seeing there a secondary episode, it must be seen as the *key* to the situation. By sowing this doubt, this deliberate ambiguity concerning the facts, it ensured that the truth about this death, and the death itself, became fascinating. Everyone exhausted himself in argument and in attempts at clarification – clarifications reinforced by the theatricality of the event which acts as a gigantic dissuasion of the terrorists' execution – everyone, and above all the revolutionaries who wanted strongly to have it that Baader had been 'assassinated'. They, too, were vultures of the truth. What's the bloody difference, anyway – suicides or victims of liquidation? The difference, of course, is that if they were liquidated and it can be proven, then the masses, guided by the truth of the facts, would know that the German State is fascist, and would mobilize in order to wreak revenge. What a load of rubbish. A death is romantic or it is not. And in the latter case, there is no need for revenge; it is of the imaginary order. What nonsense to fall back into the reality of a contract of revenge and equivalence! The avengers are worth the moralists: always evaluate the price, and have the just price paid. It matters little that the 'reality' of this death (the truth about ...) is stolen from you, since it is not of the order of the real, and therein lies its force. You are the one who depreciates it by wanting to institute it as a fact, as capital with the value of death, and to exhaust it in death, whereas this death at full price, not liquidated in the equivalence of meaning, and vengeance, opens a cycle of vertigo in which the system itself can only come to be implicated in the end, or brutally, through its own death. Such is the inspired manoeuvre of the German government, which consists in delivering through its 'calculated' errors an unfinished product, an irrecoverable truth. Thus everyone will exhaust himself finishing the work, and going to the end of the truth. A subtle incitement to self-management. It is content to produce an event involving death; others will put the finishing touches on the job. The truth. Even among the very ones who revolt at Baader's death, no one sees through this trap, and all function with the same automatism on the fringe of open complicity which all intelligent power contrives to spread around its decisions.

Far from harming Baader, the flaws of Stammheim stem from a strategy of simulation by the German State which alone would merit analysis and denunciation. A strategy of sacred union, and not at all moral, against the terrorist violence, but, much more profoundly, *a sacred union in the production of truth*, of the facts, of the real. Even if this truth explodes (if in fifteen years it is finally established that Baader was coldly liquidated), it will hardly be a scandal. No power will be frightened by it; if necessary, the crew of leaders will be changed. The price of the truth for power is superficial. On the other hand, the benefits of general mobilization, dissuasion, pacification, and mental socialization obtained through this crystallization of the truth are immense. A smart operation, under which Baader's death threatens to be buried indefinitely.

Translated by Paul Foss, Paul Patton, and John Johnstone

Note

Originally published in *In the Shadow of the Silent Majorities ... Or the End of the Social, And Other Essays*, New York: Semiotext(e), 1983, pp. 113–23.

PART V

IRONIC AESTHETIC DISORDERS

Barbara Kruger

Like utopia, all the utopias of the nineteenth and twentieth centuries, by becoming real, have driven reality from reality, leaving us in a hyper-reality devoid of meaning because meaning and the finality of reality have become absorbed and digested. The only residue of reality is a surface without depth, but with an intense superficial energy that suffices to propel the fragments of reality into a different orbit. No one knows what mysterious gravitational pull still links the scattered fragments of reality. Perhaps technology alone preserves a constellation of meaning and reality. By the same token, irony has passed into things. It is no longer a critical function, a mirror reflecting the uncertainty, the probable absurdity, of the world. Today, irony is inherent in things, it has become an *objective* irony. The instant things become man-made products, artefacts, signs, commodities, they perform an artificial and ironic function by their very existence, whose origin is transparent. We no longer have to project irony into a natural world; we no longer need an external mirror that offers the world the image of its double. Our universe has swallowed its double. It has therefore become spectral, transparent. And the irony of this embodied double bursts out continually, in every parcel of our signs, in every detail of our models. We no longer have to do what the surrealists did: juxtapose objects with the absurdity of their functions, in a poetic unreality. Objects now take it upon themselves to become clear ironically, all by themselves. Things discard their meaning effortlessly. We no longer have to underscore artifice or nonsense; they are part of the very depiction of things, part of their visibility.

Today, all things are doomed to appearance. Having no origin and deriving from a few general modes, things have no secret. They are condemned to publicity, to making themselves believable, to being seen and promoted. Our modern world is one of publicity in its very essence (or rather in its transparency). One would think it was invented solely to be publicized in a different world. We should not believe that publicity came *after* commodities. In the very heart of merchandise (and, by extension, in the very heart of our entire universe of signs), there is *an evil genius of advertising*, a trickster who has integrated the buffoonery of merchandise with its *mise-en-scène*, its staging. An ingenious scriptwriter (perhaps capital itself) has pulled the world into a phantasmagoria, and we are all its spellbound victims.

Today, all things want to be manifested. Technological, industrial, and media objects, indeed, all sorts of artefacts, even natural objects, wish to signify, to be seen, read, recorded, photographed. You only think you are photographing a scene or a landscape. In fact, the scene or landscape *wishes* to be photographed. It determines you; you are merely a supernumerary in its staging, secretly moved by the self-publicizing perversion of the surrounding world. That is the irony – I might almost be tempted to say the *pataphysical* irony – of the situation. Metaphysics is actually swept away by this reversal of the situation: the subject is no longer at the origin of the process; it is merely the agent of the objective irony of the world. Barbara Kruger might offer I'LL NOT BE YOUR MIRROR as the epitaph for this veritable subversion of the traditional universe, for this new order, or ironic disorder, of things. WE WILL NO LONGER BE YOUR FAVOURITE DISAPPEARING ACT. A defensive statement, I would personally rather shift into offensive terms: YOU WILL BE OUR FAVOURITE DISAPPEARING ACT! YOU WILL BE OUR MIRROR. This would illustrate the ironic and triumphant revenge of the object rather than the unfortunate revolt of the subject.

But this is only a manner of speaking. The message conveyed by these images is never a true message. Luckily for us, I might add. For if the weight of the words were to be added to the shock of the photos, the totality would be a semantically unbearable redundancy. Hence, text and photo designate one another ironically. Behind these images there are overtones of Magritte's formula: 'Ceci n'est pas une pipe' (This is not a pipe). The text says 'This photo is not a photo', but at the same time the photo says 'This text is not a message'. This means what it means, but this (the political, feminist, ideological message) cannot be made to speak unless it is isolated from the whole, and that would be unfair and dishonest. For we would then have nothing but naïve prophecies or banal stereotypes. The singularity of these images is that the text (which we seize upon first, in accordance with an old mental tradition of reading) is instantly short-circuited by the image, which, for its part, cannot help ceasing to impose itself as total visual evidence or as truth because it is intercepted and diverted by the text. Neither is the key to the other. The text and the photo function together in order to produce a real image – not by mutual reinforcement but by annulling and foiling one another. It is the internal irony, the subtle contradiction slipping in among the elements of the montage, that makes the montage aesthetically readable. And it is the disaccumulation, not the accumulation, of meaning that makes us accomplices of the image. Incidentally, this irony is sharpened by the almost surrealistic exorbitance of the montage.

In all these images, the photo and the message are exaggerated, making the images seem like scholarly or medical panels designed to explain the physiology or pathology of a society to the children, the handicapped, or the deaf-mutes of ideology. They are almost tactile images for the blind. No doubt this reveals that we have truly become societies with a weak ideological sensibility, a weak capacity of reading – societies diminished in meaning and in the perception of meaning, handicapped with regard to meaning. Hence, we can alert minds not with subtle hieroglyphs but with Mad[ison] Ave hieroglyphs, whose overblown nature exposes our situation. Likewise, the continual admonishment by means of the YOU, the WE, the I, the categorical imperative of the personal pronoun, exposes a society with a weak identity. The YOU, the I, the WE, are designated only by an antiphrasis, which in itself is violently ironic because it addresses authorities that are now disappearing. I do not believe that these images create a collective mobilization or awareness. If they have such a political goal, they would be naïve (as naïve as advertising when it believes it is delivering a message, whereas nowadays any text whatsoever is read *as an image*). These images create not an ideological depth but an ironic depth, by means of the injunction of the YOU and its repetition, which actually emphasize the absence of the other, of the interlocutor – or at least his problematical presence. This is the litany of a society of communication which does not *itself* communicate, in which the medium exists, all media exist, but not a single message can be deciphered collectively. Or rather, all messages exist, fully available, but there is no one at the other end of the sign. A society in which one desperately tries to speak to someone – but who?

That is how I would interpret this vehement feminine addressing of the masculine, or vehement interpellation of power, all powers that be: I AM YOUR IMMACULATE CONCEPTION. WE ARE YOUR CIRCUMSTANTIAL EVIDENCE. For does something masculine still exist to answer, does any power still exist to reply? Is there still enough of a sexual difference for antagonistic communication to exist? And what good can it do to make the masculine admit – when it no longer has the strength – that it is the masculine? The masculine can respond only by vanishing, which it has already done. And then what? By the same token, is there still such a thing as a power relationship, a political contradiction strong enough to produce a radical and antagonistic challenge to power? And what advantage could there be in forcing power to admit that it is *power* at the very moment when it no longer has the means or political energy?

Thus the virtue of these images resides, no doubt, not in political demystification or provocation but in designating the absence of either the virtual antagonist or the masses and thereby underlining the unreality of our state of things. By exaggerating the recipient's goal, these images reflect the unconsummated marriage of communication, the blank writing of a politics of the image. That is why the medium decomposes into a montage; the medium itself no longer believes in the true coherence of its own message. This does not make it lose all its power. It maintains its superior power of irony, and it bears witness to its rage to signify even when there is nothing left to say. THE MEDIUM IS BEAUTIFUL.

Another thing I like about these images (images?) is their virtual relationship to the surrounding space. One can imagine them in just about any size: miniaturized as decals or stencils or graffiti (they could even be turned into postcards), or blown up as posters or enormous billboards in the heart of a city or sky writing on a screen of clouds. Or, of course, one can imagine them in a gallery or museum. But even in such an exhibition they would denote all other sizes. They are actually mobile orbital images meant to describe space (including interior space) rather than to occupy the fixed space of conventional art. They no longer have the constraints of the (aesthetic) proscenium; instead, they have the new freedom of the movie screen. They cannot be isolated from one another; they form a chain reaction. They are like a continuous *orbit* of reflecting panels that mirror our 'exorbitant' modern condition. They disengage themselves from a frame line, from any rigorous localizing, as well as from the determined mode of vision that is part of the aesthetic definition of art (which still exercises great control over our present-day depictions). Now, at last, they regain something of the strength and immediacy of forms before, or after, the aestheticization of our culture. One can see them either as advertising, pure and simple, as advertising images that are *almost* superficial and stereotypical, or as quasi-primitive masks that, beyond their aesthetic quality (which is only attributed to them subsequently, or which they never attain), live from the intensity of the phantasms or exorcisms they induce. Just like masks, these images perform a kind of *exorcism* on our society. Like masks, which absorb the identities of actors, dancers, and spectators, and whose function is thereby to provoke something like a thaumaturgic (traumaturgic) vertigo, I believe that these images have a force and function to absorb the inter-locutor (YOU) and send him reeling, rather than to communicate. Somewhat like those fascinating faces for which the written text would be their eyes and gaze – absorption and rejection, exactly as in exorcistic and paroxysmal forms. Kruger's images thus completely reflect the society we live in – a society of paroxysm and exorcism, that is, a society in which we have absorbed our own reality and our own identity to a dizzying degree and now try to reject them forcefully, a society in which all reality has absorbed its double to a dizzying degree and now tries to expel it in all its forms.

Translated by Joachim Neugroschel

Note

Originally published as 'Untitled', in *Barbara Kruger*, New York: Mary Boone and Michael Werner, 1987, no page numbers. This essay was written on the occasion of a Kruger exhibition in May 1987.

Olivier Mosset

The Object that is None

To speak of abstraction, as with any other thing today, presupposes a distinction between an original and 'heroic' form of abstraction and a secondary, derivative, neo, or retro form – whichever term is of little importance. 'Primary' abstraction, whether it be expressionist or geometric, is part and parcel of the history of painting: the deconstruction of representation and the destruction of the object. It still relates to a subject, but ventures to pursue it to the far reaches where it begins to disintegrate. The secondary form lies one step beyond disintegration. While primary abstraction evinces a break with (and possibly the end of) the history of painting, the other is no longer inscribed by catastrophic convulsion; rather, its field is that of indifference and banality. This is, without a doubt, true as well for figuration and, in this sense, second- (or third-) generation abstraction is essentially no different than Pop Art or Superrealism. Just as these genres seize upon the most mundane aspects of everyday life and take as their subject banal images which are so ordinary or habitual that they go virtually unnoticed, so secondary abstraction retraces (with a minimum of effort) the formalization or the total disincarnation of our world, no longer in its dramatic but in its banal phase. The abstract painting of our world is nothing new – as all forms of art of an indifferent world carry the same stigmata of indifference. This is intended neither as denigration nor as depreciation, but as the state of things. To be authentic and relevant, painting must be as indifferent to itself as the world to which it belongs has become. Its essential values played, replayed and faded into oblivion, the phenomenon of its own disappearance, by now habitual, exists prior to all subsequent action. Will this dedramatized simulation perpetuate itself *ad infinitum*? Whatever forms it may take, we are certainly stranded indefinitely in the psychodrama of disappearance and transparency. We must not delude ourselves by a false sense of the continuity of painting and its history. Olivier Mosset, I think, is not one to be deluded. Here we are in complicity. What I question is the necessity for such painting – I speak of the object, of the product, and not of the individuality of the painter. But then Mosset would retort: 'And where is the need for writing, in a field of thought where the lack of differentiation is at least as great?' It is true that necessity restricts itself more and more, be it the act of painting or of writing, to the dimension of chance, a random act without reverberation, an action which, taken to the limit, will concern no one but the 'creator'. Not that it is entirely devoid of meaning for him: a discourse may very well illustrate or subtitle it (saying as often as not what he does not say and does not want to say). What is lacking, however, is the symbolic space of the viewer's gaze.

It is very difficult to speak of painting today, because there is great difficulty in seeing it. It is as though painting – in particular, New Geometric Abstraction – does not wish to be regarded and does not regard you. This is true in every way – including the annotation that it does not concern you in that it does not seek to concern you. It constitutes, as it were, the most economical, the most elliptical, the most allusive form of exchange possible. Fundamentally, the most accurate account of this discourse is that it is one in which there is nothing to say – an exact equivalent of a painting in which there is nothing to see. The equivalent of an object that is none. (While the greater part of this discourse constructs or pretends to construct an object in reference to itself or in reference to others, and at the same time substitutes itself for them, it creates a pseudo-mental and pseudo-intellectual field, revealing the cannibalizing instinct of our milieu while concealing the 'real' problem.) Thus, an object that is none, a painting that is none, a form that is none (the repetition of a circle, or stripe, or point), a colour that is none. In the monochrome, in spite of the narcissistic game of subtle differences and tonalities, there is still the question of colour that is none since it disdains the play of difference. Quite to the contrary, colour enters the vast field of indifference; it plays with the paroxysms of indifference in that it does not 'regard' you. All this is not nothingness. An object that is not an object is not nothing. It is a pure object which doesn't cease to obsess us with its own immanence, its empty and material presence. The whole problem is at the limit of nothingness to materialize nothingness; at the limit of the void to trace the filigree of the void; at the limit of indifference to play according to the mysterious roles of indifference.

Am I not myself, at this instant, in the process of filling this void, of fabricating a significant nothingness? But, of course. It is necessary to abandon a pure object to its own destiny; otherwise, it will avenge itself. And when I see such paintings 'that are none', I tell myself that this 'new' geometric abstraction is, in a way, an instrument of vengeance, something which, without shedding blood, without shedding signs, ridicules all the ambient pathos of signs and messages, of violence and blood (including the violence of interpretation) that give 'meaning' to our life and to our pseudo-reality. In the same way that a witticism, in its nonsensical and elliptical forms, ridicules all the heavy armature of language and communication. Within this is a *jouissance* and its irony entraps us in the impossible interaction between the painting and the viewer. We owe a debt of gratitude to some, including Olivier Mosset, for having maintained this very delicate balance without yielding to the nostalgic charm of painting; for having maintained this subtle line, which, to tell the truth, is less akin to aestheticism and more to setting up a decoy. It is a strategy which must not and cannot avow its true nature: a strategy of thwarted exchange which deludes the senses, and which is, ultimately, perhaps the inheritance of that ritual tradition which has never truly merged with painting – that of *trompe l'oeil*.

Translated by Hans Eberstark and Jan Avgikos

Note

Originally published as 'L'objet qui n'en est pas un', in *Olivier Mosset* [Catalogue published for the exhibition at the Swiss Pavilion as part of the Venice Biennale, 1990], Bern: Bundesamt für Kultur, 1990.

Enrico Baj, or Monstrosity Laid Bare by Paint Itself

'No player can be greater than the game itself'. This is the symbolic rule dictating that the final stakes and rules of the game escape the player no matter how great. It sums up, in a sense, the adventurous spirit of Baj at work.

Constellated with festoons, decorations, starry fragments of mirror, and scattered signs, these paintings display Baj's virtuosity. He plays with these signs at random, endowing them with some of the humour and freedom they have lost in being used as signals. He plays humourously with his material, wielding a kind of thick humour inherent in the material proper of painting, the texture itself becoming satirical. For example, consider the series of generals or women: figures and forms, ultra-bodies, as it were, carved in an ironically decorative texture, primitively ringed with thick black lines like the lips of larval dragonflies, or the soft excrescences of unicellular, almost undifferentiated, creatures reproducing themselves by contiguity. Upon this textured substructure of a world that has reverted to larvae and masks blink the signs of belated decay either of the superannuated and satiated bourgeoisie or the endless debris of our modern consumer society. The spangle or the badge are, each in its own way, signs of an all-powerful conformism which become, thanks to the beauty of the painting, the signs of its decomposition. In Baj's painting there is also a strange superimposition of ponderous immobile violence – that of the material, line, and assemblage – and a sarcastic violence in the baroque mirror of grimacing signs. Though surrealistic in effect, it is not an intellectual surrealism, agile and critical, the short-circuit between ideas and their representation, between object and function, to which we are accustomed. Nor is it a cerebral intellectuality where dream closely approaches idea. In Baj's case what we have is a kind of telescoping, a crashing against each other of two materialities: a crude material half-way between metamorphic rock, cell plasma, and larvae, and that, just as crude, despite appearances, of signs and their mockery.

This is the secret of Baj's monstrosity. That is, the monstrous is the fact of the pictorial event itself and not merely characteristic of what it represents; happily for Baj, and happily for painting as well, for it is at this juncture that the game outstrips the players. The raw material of monstrosity and the work of signs of monstrosity far exceed the historical figures of Fascist generals just as the monstrous job of painting far outstrips the social-historical goal of designation or denunciation which it might have set itself. Baj speaks of his generals in terms of the 'progressive personification of specific raw material'. But isn't it rather the opposite? Isn't it the historical brutality of the generals, which, as such, is only of intellectual interest, not in itself monstrous (for monstrosity is not simple brutality nor simple violence, but has a sacred character), transmuted in Baj's case into a veritable brutality of painting, into a brutality of signs themselves (or the reverberation of a material in the grotesque mirror of signs) that painting alone can achieve? Suddenly this monstrosity describes, at one and the same time, the wretched, despicable monstrosity of the generals, and that which transcends it, the savage, subversive primitive and sacred monstrosity that cuts through the social order by means of signs of totalitarian hyperconformism.

This is of course highly ambiguous, but the ambiguity is part of the monstrosity; indeed, it is its aesthetic ferment. Moreover, in a system of production and consumption which exists through the transparency of its signals and the terrorism of its transparency, only ambiguous signs are revolutionary. The generals are ambiguous, not in our minds nor in Baj's protest (here, they are out-and-out odious), but in his painting, where, contrary to all logic, they assume the mythical dimensions of primitive masks. This mythical dimension, monstrous in the sublime sense of the term, can just as well be discovered in a piece of furniture, in an ultra-body, in the shattering of a mirror or in the monotony of a series. Only painting which succeeds in being itself a monstrous act succeeds in resolving and in reabsorbing the monstrosity of our lives. Only painting that succeeds in becoming a mythic operator also succeeds in resolving the monstrosity of the social and of the social order. And in this Baj's painting succeeds admirably.

Note

Originally published as 'Baj ou la monstruosité mise à nu par la peinture même', in *Enrico Baj*, Paris: Filipacchi, 1980, pp. 10–12. The English translation was also included in this edition, without indicating the name of the translator.

The Transparency of Kitsch

A *Conversation with Enrico Baj*

Jean Baudrillard: Why the German title *Die Mythologie des Kitsches*?[1]

Enrico Baj: 'Kitsch' comes from the German, and for my latest show in Italy I thought I'd use it in its linguistic context. I've stressed the kitsch aspect by including exotic wild animals like lions, tigers, and snakes, as well as tropical vegetation. It's a kind of tribute to Douanier Rousseau; the imagery is occasionally allegorical.

JB: You call all that kitsch?

EB: Since the turn of the century, we've seen extraordinary avant-garde movements: the anarchic expressionism of Die Brücke, Futurism, Dada, Geometric Abstraction. But no one single style ever managed to attract universal support. The end result was a mix, a blending of styles.

JB: No specific style took the lead because there was no longer a coherent, collective perception of things. Instead, there was a sort of division and subdivision of the perceptual system. You can see this everywhere, be it in politics or aesthetics. It's a kind of polymorphous dispersion of ideologies and opinions.

EB: Kitsch crops up in all facets of life. But it's possibly more conspicuous in art, because in art there's perhaps a greater claim to stylistic coherence.

JB: Yes, because art is visualization. It's a very strong reflex action, not at all like writing. Art is a sort of eye-opener. But I think the problems are the same all over. It has nothing to do with the avant-garde being finished. It's the art cycle that's come full circle. Anticipation is no longer a possibility. Did you ever get the impression you were part of the avant-garde?

EB: I've definitely been part of it, yes. First, back in 1951, in the anti-nuclear movement. Then with Jorn in 1953, when we made a stand against the rationalization of art and the invasion of geometry, the line, and the right angle. We founded a movement that foreshadowed the Situationist International. My first contacts with the Lettrists were in 1952 and 1954. I used to get their bulletin *Potlatch*. But I didn't like the politicized language they used. They had a sort of Stalinist style crammed with accusations and self-criticism, with admissions of all sorts of treachery.

JB: The avant-garde is like a secret police force.

EB: People claim the avant-garde phenomenon lasted until Pop. But Pop soon lost its experimental innovative aspect.

JB: I wouldn't even take it as far as Pop. But Abstract Expressionism was still a kind of avant-garde. Avant-gardes are subversive, and Abstract Expressionism was still a form of gestural subversion of painting and representation. After that, we're no longer talking about the avant-garde. It's still possible to come up with something new, but this is merely 'posthumous representation'. It's beyond the destruction of representation. What's more, this creates a very confused world, because all forms are possible. In this sense it may be true that beyond the avant-garde you simply have kitsch. Pop is kitsch. But so are new abstract painting, new representational painting, Bad painting, and so on.

EB: The kitsch of modern production, with monuments erected in its honour. In the early days of Pop there was still an ironical, critical dimension.

JB: I don't think there was any critical subversion in Pop. Nor any real irony, either. Pop is about something different. It's more paradoxical.

EB: You've used the term 'subversion'. The avant-garde isn't opposed to things only on a formal level: it confronts and opposes officialdom. The Impressionists didn't really produce an aggressive manifesto. They didn't take up any definite stand. But in the way they lived and in their works they were against officialdom. They were against contemporary taste and aesthetics. They opposed the turgid academic art that represented and celebrated power and authority. In my opinion, what you see nowadays in certain important museums is once again turgid conventional art. Usually it's 'installations' which are bombastic monuments to contemporary taste. The new academicism is based broadly on a penchant for materials, which are exploited over and over again, in certain examples of *arte povera*, for instance, or in series of images like Warhol's *Campbell's Soup* and *Coca Cola*.

JB: The new conventionality isn't religious, historical, allegorical, or ceremonial. It comes from somewhere lower down the scale, from banality and the humdrum. In a quantitative sense, there's always been the same volume of academic art. But today it is masked by banality, by the 'exquisite corpse' of banality. Conventional art was ostracized, and is now making its triumphant return, revived by the present-day mania for bringing back everything. Where present-day art is concerned, it has become extremely difficult to make judgements. There's no aesthetic criterion any more.

EB: It's always been difficult to make judgements. 'Conventional' means something that's nicely polished and varnished and shiny, something that doesn't rock the boat. All those big Conceptual and Minimalist American things, they're nicely polished and lacquered. Even raw and natural elements are glorified in installations by the use of clever lighting and spacing. These effects make an installation clean, hygienic, and dazzling.

JB: Conventional art has to look clean. There's such a demand from museums and from the public at large for sanctifying anything and everything. And it's precisely this cultural demand that's kitsch. There's another kind of kitsch, too: the kitsch of traditional popular art that doesn't really hang on aesthetics, so much as on craftmanship. It is kitsch in relation to art, but it has an originality of its own. Kitsch is a pathological outgrowth of aesthetics. And today it's produced by the institution of aesthetics, no less. You yourself have retained control over what you do. In your work there's a form of exploration and invention that's true to itself. You haven't been caught up in the pathological circuit. I don't know how artists ever find their way around it.

EB: Carl Andre once said about Warhol that, for better or worse, we got the artist we deserved. To which I replied: 'The artist *you* deserved, maybe'. As far as I'm concerned, I won't put up with any kind of identification with Warhol. And it must be said that there's a whole range of verdicts, not just Carl Andre's.

JB: It used to be possible to work within the secrecy of tradition, outside the market. It was still possible to have a different way of looking at things. Nowadays this seems very difficult to do. Can a work be subversive toward the very market that has publicized that work? Is it possible to stand up to conformity, to the dictatorship of the market, to value systems, to the powers that be? For example, the demographic basis of your pictures raises a general, worldwide, human problem. Do you think that over and above their visual force they might help to change things? Nobody is in control of the world's population; in a way it's man's inexorable fate. You can fight political powers quite openly, but the population problem is beyond our grasp. What are you criticizing in your painting? Is your painting more than a dramatic illustration of a problem?

EB: I intend to go on taking stances and giving my works meanings that go beyond aesthetic values. The problem of the population explosion, which is the subject of *Seven Billion by the Year 2000*, conjures up another danger: the mass popularization of art. From something inviting reflection and contemplation, art has become a mass phenomenon that has nothing to do with art. The horde quashes any chance of perceiving aesthetic phenomena. All the artist can do is live and work in the solitude of his studio, unless he decides to turn his studio into a factory. Painting is not some kind of theatre, as people would have it today. Art is nurtured by solitude and silence. The masses do not produce visions and thoughts and dreams. They turn things that weren't into kitsch. Look at the Mona Lisa with her moustache and the caption 'L.H.O.O.Q'. Here it's Duchamp (and Picabia) interpreting the transformation of a masterpiece by the masses.

JB: I'd say that the masses are the supreme kitsch product. At the same time the masses are a mirror of power that has itself become kitsch. So we're no longer talking about subversion by the masses. We're talking about a disqualification of power by its extension to the masses. When power ventures into the realm of statistics, it loses all specificity. This produces a sort of perverse contract between power and the masses, a mutually manipulative contract. Your painting dealing with demographic catastrophe and overpopulation is also addressing the problem of overcrowding in the art world; overinformation and overcommunication are like cancerous proliferations. Can this trend be stopped? You are still trying. But in the meantime things have become destabilized. You think you are at the hub of a system of subversion and radical criticism; but, in subtle ways, you no longer know where you are. When painting tries to put across an idea, it brings the present-day fate of ideologies upon itself.

EB: We have entered a permanent crisis.

JB: Right. But I know people who don't relate this crisis to painting. For them, painting has become a kind of sanctuary, a refuge for traditional know-how.

EB: As a rule I like painting to be connected with things and events that affect people. Ten years ago you saw my Milan show on the theme of the *Apocalypse*.[2] Your own mind is often apocalyptic, if you'll forgive the expression. Your intelligence enables you to penetrate pretence, semblances, and the mediatization of art. This process of mediatization has already, to a large degree, replaced both reality and life. In any event, as far as I'm concerned, there's no question of me turning in on myself. On the contrary, I want to be alive and kicking, the better to fight the fight and suggest solutions. This might seem ridiculous, but I've got lots of confidence in imagination, invention and dreams. I'm hopeful both on my own account, and for other people too. I think we'll come through the current situation, which is flat, agnostic, indifferent, and unmotivating. This is something Freud didn't reckon on – people without drive, people unable to change direction.

JB: I can see both sides. Sometimes I think there's an irreversible move toward non-desire – a withdrawal from desire. Warhol's part of this, but he's not the only one. You can see this happening in society, in the demise of political passions, in the history of events that are no longer events. You can see it in the whole gamut of things that it's no longer possible for people to desire or imagine. You can describe this as a fatal, irreversible development. Yet at the same time, you can imagine that something different will come about. But what? History teaches us that there's a succession of civilizations and cultures, and that, in the end, something new invariably occurs. But some cultures have completely vanished. So catastrophe is a possibility – catastrophe in the apocalyptic sense of the term, which has nothing to do with crisis. I mean a catastrophe in the sense of a process of acceleration, an accelerated unravelling of forms. The whole theory of chaos charts a revolution of forms that is accidental rather than critical. Forms aren't revived by nature. They're revived by their movement through catastrophe, by extreme phenomena. You yourself trust in Good, in the indestructible vitality of nature, and in desire. I'm less confident than you. I tend to believe that catastrophe will bring the system to a point where it'll explode. I have no illusions and no certainty about what might happen afterwards. But I make suppositions about going to extremes and in some ways precipitating the motions. When you yourself depict the apocalypse, or the population crisis, you're imagining the worst.

EB: I'm imagining a certain vitality that's a sort of hope. I believe in the power of imagination. That doesn't stop me from seeing the worst. But I don't see the acceleration of the worst as a preferable solution. Even if we're living in a situation of tedium and dull acceptance of things, how can you hope that we won't get out of it? Are we meant simply to sit and wait for our final destruction?

JB: There are various solutions, and I find Warhol's position particularly interesting, when he holds up the mirror of a utopia based on sheer banality. It's a bit like what I do when I push concepts to their limit in order to incite a violent abreaction. I'm not looking for progressive, positive action any more. I'm looking for negative or paradoxical abreaction, in extreme phenomena. From here on, it's a strategy of provocation, not invocation. Invocation involves utopia and make-believe. Warhol interests me because he develops a media-oriented, mechanical strategy. It's consistent with the strategy of the system, but faster than the system itself. It doesn't dispute the system, but it pushes it to the point of absurdity, by overdoing its transparency.

EB: It's only scientists and people concerned with these problems who make catastrophic forecasts of an irreversible destruction that won't lead to another form of socio-cultural reorganization.

JB: Right. It's a bigger risk because it's a poker game, a game of outbidding. Whereas the other is a more human, more rational prospect. It, too, leads to catastrophe, but in an underhanded way. And nothing will re-emerge from this slow-motion catastrophe.

EB: We're talking about art and people and anthropology. But let's be frank: does our chum Warhol interest us more than nuclear weapons and pollution and worldwide desertification?

JB: Do you hold out any hope for ecology?

EB: I'm not exactly hopeful. But all the same, you can't ignore the pollution that's all around us – in the air, in economics, in politics, and even in art. This pollution is caused by distorting the meaning of things. You saw how terminological and aesthetic confusion won the day at the last Biennale. France exhibited architectural projects. The sculpture prize went to photos. The prize for artists under thirty-five was given to someone older, and so on and so forth. And what about Jenny Holzer's 'truisms'?

JB: It's really macabre. But you're quite right. Pollution is not just in our air and water. It's also present in the promiscuity and confusion of genres and styles. It is caused by the proliferation, in the guise of art, of anything and everything. But putting any old thing on display is taking people for a ride. It's blackmail based on insecurity (of judgement and pleasure), and that's not acceptable. The art scene is a spectacle, a show. This means things are degenerating. It's pretty obvious that there's no real space left for painting. What's left is a sort of happening. Times have changed. This is a very ephemeral period. It's not a period of painting. It has much more to do with other forms of expression: photography, cinema, audiovisual media, electronics. From now on, this is what art's about. The museum and the happening at one and the same time – things that are utterly contradictory and yet in cahoots.

EB: And what about those exhibition catalogues? So heavy …

JB: The catalogue is a performance. An exhaustive performance that can often substitute for the exhibition.

EB: The catalogue for a great exhibition also has another function: that of offering options, like the catalogues of optional extras that you get with cars. In painting you have the option of Jenny Holzer and Jeff Koons; architects or painting since the French architecture pavilion at the Biennale was given over to paintings. You can also choose between Olivier Mosset and Elsworth Kelly. The option, the accessory, is a good producer of kitsch. A car is kitsch enough as it is. If you added all those optional extras you'd get something quite monstrous; you've probably seen the air bags that Mercedes Benz has developed. In the event of a collision, the bag inflates and prevents you from getting impaled on the steering wheel. Clearly it has to inflate before impact.

JB: You can very easily imagine it inflating afterwards and suffocating the driver.

EB: We've talked about kitsch, of the masses that thrive on it the way they thrive on dictators and rock stars, but art auctions are part of the same phenomenon. Selling Van Gogh to the Japanese is a kind of financial kitsch. There's also mystical and minimal kitsch. I met a collector who had a whole corridor given over to an installation of Philips neon lights by Dan Flavin. When the neon fired, the collector saw divine transcendence in the purity of the cold light. I saw the reflection of God in his eyes. The age of purity started with Malevich. His experiments prompted a protracted discourse: is it better to have a white square on a white background, a white square on a black background, or a black square on a black background? Here already one achieves a sublimation of kitsch. Malevich did the black on white in 1915. It took him another three years to get to the white on white; this leisurely pace is what is needed to transform purity into something operational. In such a case, purity becomes spectacle.

JB: That work contains a sort of metaphysics of the void, a compulsion to vanish. There are various ways of vanishing: by forms tapering off, by conceptualization, by see-through geometry, or else by excess, proliferation, and redundancy. As I see it, art has followed both paths. Is it still possible to talk in terms of aesthetics? If art has ever had a definition, that definition has had to do with mastering a craft, in order to provide an objective illusion of the world. Since Dada, I have not been able to see most art as art. I see it as something symptomatic of a kind of neurosis. All of a sudden, aesthetic judgement becomes secondary, because it's no longer really relevant. Added to which, I can no longer ask myself whether something's beautiful or not. As Thierry de Duve has emphasized, up to a certain point it was possible to say: 'This is beautiful, that isn't' – an aesthetic judgement. Then, at some given moment, we're no longer thinking in terms of beauty, and we say: 'This is art and that isn't'. This is an important change. But there may be a stage beyond all this where art doesn't even enter the picture. As a specific practice, art has more or less vanished. Things are already at a very advanced stage of degeneration.

EB: There's much talk about the disappearance of art. People used to talk about the death of art. In Italy you published a text about the disappearance of art – the disappearance of art in a society that hasn't yet disappeared.[3]

JB: But I'm saying that the disappearance of art is offset by the art of disappearance. In other words, this isn't the end of art, because the actual disappearance is a whole art unto itself.

EB: You add that art is not in fact obligatory. It isn't a phenomenon that must absolutely exist. If art disappeared, this wouldn't cause irreversible harm.

JB: We know that some cultures have existed quite happily on a non-aesthetic basis. But I don't think we've had any examples, to date, of a culture where art existed and then vanished, and that culture moved on to another mode. I find the idea quite fascinating. What is a society where an aesthetic base provides a system of powerful values, a system that has taken up where sacrificial systems left off? What becomes of a society like this if it loses its symbolic points of reference? Do things revert to the status quo ante, or are subsequent forms developed? I don't really have the answer. It's really an anthropological problem. Maybe we are this future type of society. Roger Caillois identifies four kinds of game: the mimetic game, the sporting/competitive game, the game of vertigo, and the game of chance. Western aesthetics is a mimetic game of expression, a game of representation. It's also a game of challenge: challenge to the real world and to the expression of the real world. But it's possible to make up random, or vertiginous, games – different forms of games that depend on different sensibilities, and on different types of action. Maybe we're in the process of moving from a culture of expression and competition to vertiginous or random societies.

EB: We've talked about the disappearance of art, or, rather, the art of disappearance. We've talked about the non-necessity of art, and the possible shift from an aesthetic society to a non-aesthetic or 'transaesthetic' one. The fact is, the mass of people I portray in my pictures could also be the mass of painting and painters. There are an incredible number of painters out there.

JB: A galloping demography, a spontaneous multiplication like that of germs. In the face of such a fabulous expansion in the supply, it is not clear where the demand might be. It is always the same problem: aspiration is as problematic as inspiration. People consume art, they devour it. But we will never know whether they really needed it or whether they wanted it. In any event they are not given the choice. In the extreme, everyone will become creators and then everyone will be on the supply-side. Will there still be consumers?

EB: After the war, at the time of COBRA and the last avant-garde movement in Italy, very little was sold, and artists often swapped canvases among themselves. We could therefore reach a point of constant exchange which could lead to an obligatory trans-aesthetic circulation.

JB: This would no longer be a question of market-based circulation, it would be a kind of 'potlatch', and that would effectively be the transaesthetic realization of things. Unfortunately, it could also end up in a massive bottleneck.

EB: But there would always be galleries that could act as traffic lights and, over and above policing the traffic, they could always provide paintings to those who had been excluded from the 'potlatch' but wanted, nonetheless, to take part.

JB: Speaking in terms of supply and demand means that the laws of the market have already been accepted. The cultural postulate is that the demand is constantly increasing, that more and more art is needed. That is not proven. In any event, there is nothing in art that resembles a democratic exercise. It is not true that everyone should have some, nor that man has any cultural rights. For aesthetic enjoyment, aesthetic judgement, to endure, there has to be a secret complicity, a closeted dimension. Now we see clearly that the supply is constantly increasing, that the creators are becoming legion, and they feed the circuits that are becoming ever more voracious. But where is the demand, what does it become? Everyone goes to see everything. There is a statistical drain: 300,000 people went to see a Warhol show. That's wonderful, but we will never know what they expected to see, nor if they actually saw anything.

That remains a mystery. If art has a function today, it remains indecipherable. What are people looking for? The destruction of culture or its absorption? In absorbing it, they destroy it. They come to gobble up Beaubourg, eating up the building and what is in it at the same time. A type of extraordinary cultural cannibalism. No one can get the better of it but no one is asking questions anymore, since we start from the principle that the stronger the demand, the better the thing is working. It is clear that this increases values, and creates a phenomenon of a sort of 'cultural dumping'. What has been unleashed is a kind of cultural demand that has nothing to do with aesthetics. While the aesthetic dimension seems so obvious to you, to me, to us, in our worlds, for 90 per cent of the people, aesthetics does not exist, the need for an aesthetic criterion is lacking.

EB: It exists at the level of cars though. In this case aesthetics shifts to things that really represent the symbols of everyday life.

JB: Take the generation I knew for example. Everything was so kitsch, so cheap, so petit bourgeois. That was fifty years ago, or even a hundred years ago. In the last century there has been such a massive aesthetic penetration, such a schooling on forms, that many things should have changed as a result. And yet, when you enter the universe of the vast majority of people, you find that absolutely nothing has changed in terms of taste, or discrimination. Everything is just as awful as it always was. There is no collective teaching in terms of aesthetics. There is no negative feeling about it, though, because conformity is a defence strategy.

EB: I have to say that design is even worse than the popular kitsch of the past. These days you often find the most absurd pretentions, such as aerodynamic shapes where they serve no purpose or, for example, the redundancy of some sofas and armchairs.

JB: Yes indeed, design is an intolerable presumption in most instances. In any event it is an added dimension, a theatrical supplement. Kitsch often springs directly from design, or design is the expression of kitsch, which is the same thing. The forced intrusion of aesthetics represents the decline of original forms. We need professionals everywhere to calculate the form of an object, its curvature, its volume. Nothing is left to intuition or to everyday use.

EB: What is success? What is the system? Because the success is often organized.

JB: They say that the publicity machine is omnipotent. Everyone maintains this comfortable illusion, either to denounce it or to take advantage of it.

But there is an unplanned element. While 90 per cent of the traffic is assured by the programmes, perhaps 5 per cent is still accidental.

EB: We spoke just now about the contribution of chance to success and of the welcome reserved to works of art by the public. But it is also possible to employ the accidental when creating a painting. Do you think that in the big picture of my work, chance has had a role to play?

JB: There too, there are some surprises which surprise even you. As your career has developed, there have been some changes of direction, invention of forms, in terms which we can correctly describe as accidental or catastrophic. The same thing sometimes happens in a conversation. A complete change takes place, and you realize that things went differently. And this cannot be known in advance.

EB: I think that, fundamentally, all my heads, and all my characters, look alike, but it is the accidental combination, the coincidence of the meetings that is able to determine the variation.

JB: In your later works, there is a sort of swarming, a kind of promiscuity, there is undoubtedly an element of horror. But I find that, compared to the *Generals*,[4] and the other things you were doing at that time, the form is more reconciled with itself. There is something happier about them. It could be the Day of Judgement but at the same time it is the earthly paradise. It is no longer exactly the caustic denunciation of a cynical world. I don't know if I am wrong, but there has been an evolution. Now there are bodies, and faces, while, with the *Generals*, there were only masks.

Notes

Originally published as 'The Transparency of Kitsch: A Conversation Between Jean Baudrillard and Enrico Baj', in Enrico Baj, *The Garden of Delights* [Including texts by Umberto Eco, Donald Kuspit and Jean Baudrillard], edited by Marisa de Re and Gio Marioni, Milan: Fabbri Editori, 1991, pp. 25–35.

1. *Trans. note. The Mythology of Kitsch* was the title of Baj's show at the City Museum of Varese, near Milano, Italy in 1990.

2. *Editor's note.* The painted plywood works constituting *Apocalypse* date from 1978–9.

3. *Editor's note.* The theme of the disappearance of art was discussed by Baudrillard in the late 1980s; see 'Transpolitics, Transsexuality, Transaesthetics', *in Jean Baudrillard: The Disappearance of Art and Politics*, trans. Michel Valentin, edited by W. Stearns and W. Chaloupka, New York: St. Martin's Press, 1992, pp. 9–26.

4. *Editor's note.* Baj began working on his *Generals* in 1959. He exhibited them at the Venice Biennale in 1964, the same year that American Pop Art conquered Europe.

Index

Compiled by Peter Munoz